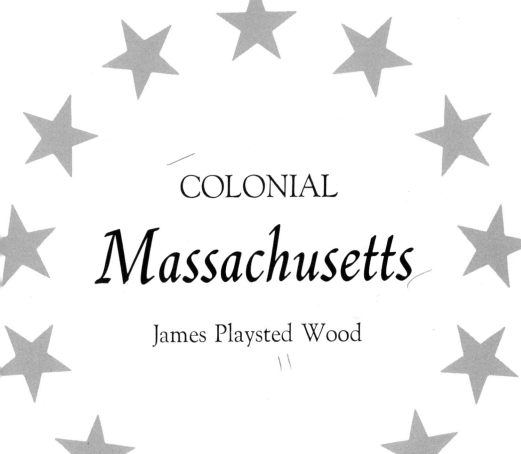

COLONIAL

Massachusetts

James Playsted Wood

Thomas Nelson

Photographs are from the following sources: Samuel Chamberlain, p. 123 (below); The Dicksons, Plymouth, Mass., pp. 22, 27 (right); Forbes Library, Northampton, Mass., pp. 33, 63, 99; Free Library of Philadelphia, (Print Room), pp. 17, 18, 21, 25, 27 (left), 32, 34-35, 37, 39, 60, 81, 120, 132, 144, 150, 155, 165; (Rare Book Department), pp. 53, 141; (Rosenbach Collection), pp. 68, 76, 137, 142; Massachusetts Chamber of Commerce, jacket back; Massachusetts Historical Society, pp. 85, 100, 114, 127; New York Metropolitan Museum of Art, p. 74; New York Public Library, Astor, Lenox and Tilden Foundations (Prints Division), jacket front, pp. 70, 159, 160-161; (Rare Book Division), p. 102; Pequot Collection, Yale University, p. 6; Pioneer Valley Association, pp. 91, 94, 123 (above); (Rodimon Collection), pp. 29, 106, 109; Plimoth Plantation, pp. 14, 16, 30; Salem Chamber of Commerce, pp. 47, 59, 77, 117; Springfield Public Library, pp. 88, 90, 97. Permission is gratefully acknowledged.

Design by Harold Leach

Library of Congress Catalog Card Number: 71-82917

Printed in the United States of America

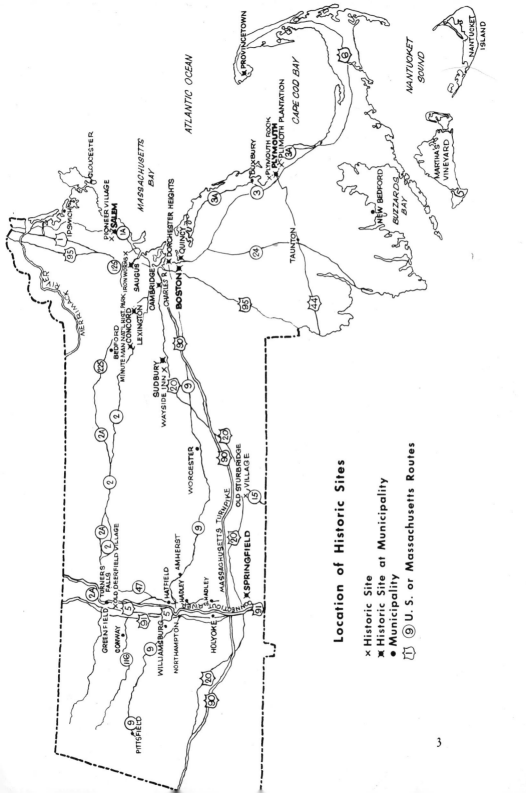

Location of Historic Sites

x Historic Site
✕ Historic Site at Municipality
● Municipality
⬡ ⑨ U. S. or Massachusetts Routes

3

Contents

INTRODUCTION

Pre-Colonial Massachusetts

Captain John Smith named Massachusetts, which means "at the long hill," for the small tribe of Algonquin Indians who lived about Boston Bay. The area had been known to Europeans for centuries before the "Pilgrims" and then the Puritans came to settle on its shores.

According to the Norse sagas of the twelfth and thirteenth centuries, Leif Eiriksson (or Ericsson) sailed from Greenland about A.D. 1001. After skirting the coasts of Labrador and Newfoundland, he and his men landed on what must have been Cape Cod where they basked in the sun and feasted on the game and fish. They named this paradise "Vinland." They returned to Greenland, but the next year Leif's brother Thorvald and a group of Norsemen returned and stayed for about two years. Thorvald was killed by the "Skraelings" or Indians.

In 1010, Thorfin Karlesfine and one hundred sixty people made at Vinland what may have been the first attempt to establish a permanent settlement in Massachusetts. They spent three years in profitable fur trading and less profitable warfare with the Indians and in quarreling among themselves before they gave up. Maps drawn by the Norsemen showed the outline of Cape Cod. The Venetian brothers Nicolo and Antonio Zeno left maps of the New England coast and an impossible account of wild adventures with the Indians there

Captain John Smith's map of 1614 shows the coast of Massachusetts. The original is in the Pequot Collection at Yale

in the sixteenth century. Juan de la Cosa, companion of Columbus, drew a map in 1500 which showed Cape Cod.

England based her claims to New England on the maps and reports of John Cabot and his son Sebastian who probably saw the coast of Massachusetts in 1509. Their reports sent the vessels of many European nations on fishing expeditions along the New England coast. It was the "Sacred Cod" of Massachusetts which brought the early fishermen and supported the first English colonists.

In 1602, Bartholomew Gosnold sailed to Cape Cod, Martha's Vineyard, and then into Buzzard's Bay, where he and his men built a hut on Cuttyhunk Island and traded with the Indians for furs, cedar, and sassafras. So profitable was the expedition and so enthusiastic were Gosnold's reports that more English ships were sent on business ventures. In 1603, Martin Pring brought the *Speedwell* and the *Discoverer* into what became Plymouth harbor where they built a barricaded tower from which sentinels watched as the crews cut and loaded sassafras. They held the natives at bay with the ships' ordnance, two great mastiffs, and a guitar. More than one hundred twenty Indians danced happily around the sailor who strummed the guitar and gave him gifts of tobacco, pipes, and snakeskin belts. When, after seven weeks, Pring and his men sailed away, hundreds of Indians paddled their canoes out to the *Discoverer* urging the Englishmen to remain.

Captain John Smith explored and mapped the New England and Massachusetts coast in 1614. He gave English names to the places he found and in *A Description of New England...*, 1616, described what seemed to him the most pleasant and promising part of the new land. He said that more profit was to be obtained from fishing its coastal waters than from all the gold London venturers had expected the Jamestown colonists to find in Virginia. He told of the great population of friendly Indians, the game, fish, fruit, the cornfields, the furs, and urged English colonization of "the Countrie of the Massachusetts, which is the Paradise of all those parts."

It was Thomas Hunt, in command of one of the ships of Smith's expedition, who kidnapped twenty Indians and sold them into slavery in Spain. Smith condemned his action as did the famed geographer Samuel Purchas, who called it "Savage hunting of Savages, a new and Devillish Project." One of the Indians whom Hunt abducted was a Wampanoag brave named Squanto who escaped from Spain to England where he remained for several years. It was this same Squanto, of course, who befriended the "Pilgrims" whose settlement at Plymouth marked the beginning of a century and a half of colonial life in Massachusetts.

It was not at all a fixed and unchanging time. As ours is, it was a time of growth and change, sometimes rapid, sometimes slow. Five generations of rich, poor, honest or dishonest, kindly or brutal, intelligent or stupid people lived and died in Massachusetts before it became a state of the United States. This is who they were, how they lived, something of what they suffered and more of what—fortunately for those who followed them—they accomplished.

J.P.W.

CHAPTER ONE

The "Pilgrims" and Plymouth Plantation

Religious toleration is a recent development. Religious beliefs were fiercely held in medieval and early Renaissance Europe, and toleration was not tolerated. The Holy Inquisition burned thousands and thousands of "heretics" at the stake in Spain and France. Nearly two thousand were burned in just one province of Spain in 1482. More thousands were put to the fire in "liberal" Netherlands in the next century. Though England was comparatively lenient, over the two centuries from Henry IV to James I about four hundred men and women went to the stake.

Henry VIII had no real love for Protestantism. It was just a personal and political convenience for him. He had men beheaded for refusing to acknowledge him head of England's state church, but he executed others for their denial of Catholic doctrine. In what was really an emerging nation's declaration of independence from Rome, England became a Protestant country but in essence remained Catholic. Queen Mary ("Bloody Mary"), daughter of Henry VIII, was a devout Catholic under whom many martyrs perished. One was Bishop Hugh Latimer, leader of the Reformation in England. As the flames leaped about him when he was burned at the stake in Oxford, October 16, 1554, he said—in words later used by William Bradford —"We shall this day light such a candle by God's grace in England as I trust shall never be put out."

Dissenters from the state Church of England were first called Lollards. They became known as "Puritans." As such, they insisted upon reading and interpreting the Bible for themselves. They believed in direct access to God through prayer rather than through the intercession of saints or the clergy. They demanded abolition of elaborate forms and ceremonies and return to the simplicity of the early Christian church. Most of the Puritans wished merely to reform and "purify" the English church. Some wished to leave it altogether and set up churches of their own. These became known as "Separatists."

The Separatists at Scrooby

Because the Church of England was a state church, the Separatists were rebelling against England. Legally they were criminals, guilty of a kind of treason, and they were prosecuted as criminals. Mobs broke up their meetings. The authorities arrested and jailed those they caught and hanged some of them. A number of the Separatists escaped into Holland.

Succeeding his father, William Brewster, who was born about January 1567, was postmaster and bailiff of Scrooby Manor in Nottinghamshire. Educated at Peterhouse College, Cambridge, where he turned to Puritanism, Brewster was a man of wealth and position who had traveled abroad on diplomatic missions. He became the leader and protector of Puritan men and women of Scrooby and nearby villages who met for worship in the drawing room of his manor. They set up what was really an independent congregational church—a church governed by its members, not by the crown.

One member of Brewster's congregation was young William Bradford who had been born in Austerfield, Yorkshire, in 1589 of a family of prosperous yeoman farmers. As the boy's father had died when the son was but a year old and his mother had married, William Bradford was brought up and taught farming by his grandfather and his uncles. He began to study the Bible when he was only twelve. Against the will of his uncles, he joined the Separatists at Scrooby Manor.

The Flight to Holland

After an investigation by the High Commission at York, the Scrooby congregation decided to avoid further interference and get away from unfriendly neighbors by flight to Holland where they would be free to worship as they pleased.

It was not an easy feat. The Separatists were forbidden by law; they were also forbidden to leave the country. In fear of both official arrest and popular violence, they had to escape England by stealth. In the fall of 1607, they hired an English ship to transport them from Boston in Lincolnshire to Amsterdam. With all their possessions, they stole aboard ship at night. Its master, who had plotted with the authorities, betrayed them to crown officers. The Separatists were put into open boats; their possessions were confiscated; men and women alike were searched for money. They were imprisoned for a month. Then all but seven who were held for trial were sent back to their villages and farms.

Daring and determined, Brewster's congregation hired a Dutch captain and his ship to transport them in the spring of 1608. They would be picked up at a large common between Grimsby and Hull. Women, children, and household goods were sent to the remote point of embarkation by a small ship, the men to join them by travel overland. So many of the women were seasick that they persuaded the skipper of their bark to put in at a creek for the night.

The next morning the Dutch ship captain began to take aboard the men who had walked along shore to the common. When he saw an armed posse coming in pursuit, he weighed anchor for Amsterdam. The men left ashore managed to escape their pursuers, but the women and children were herded together and taken before one justice after another. They were too many to imprison, and they no longer had homes to which they could be returned. The authorities knew there would be public outcry if they punished them for merely trying to follow their husbands and fathers. Finally they were allowed to leave England.

In the end, about 125 of the Scrooby congregation reached Holland. Among them were the minister John Robinson and William Brewster as well as young William Bradford. It was Bradford who first called these people "Pilgrims."

The Pilgrims stayed in Amsterdam for a year; they went then to Leyden. Here, led by Robinson and by William Brewster, who had been made an Elder, they worshiped in peace and lived in austere comfort. Simple people, learned only in the Bible, they had been farmers and artisans in England. William Brewster became a printer and publisher of Puritan books which were shipped back to England, where they could not be printed. William Bradford, who sold his inheritance in England when he came of age in 1611 and bought a house in Holland, became a fustian weaver. Most of the others obtained humble employment in the cloth trades.

By nature the Pilgrims were honest and industrious. In *Of Plymouth Plantation*, the account of his people which is one of the basic documents of American history, William Bradford says, "And first, though many of them were poor, yet there was none so poor but if they were known to be of that congregation the Dutch (either bakers or others) would trust them in any reasonable matter when they wanted money, because they had found by experience how careful they were to keep their word and saw them so painful and diligent in their callings."

What began to bother the Pilgrims was their exile itself. ". . . they heard a strange and uncouth language, and beheld the different manners and customs of the people, with their strange fashions and attires, all so far differing from that of their plain country villages (wherein they were bred and had so long lived)."

The Pilgrims were English and wished to remain so. Parents saw

Plimoth Plantation is a re-creation of the first Pilgrim village as it appeared in 1627. From the records of the first census taken in that year, it is known who lived in each of the nineteen dwellings. Governor Bradford's street layout indicated where the houses were, and how much land was allotted to each one

their children growing up in a strange land, knowing Dutch better than English, and often infected by the liberality—the Pilgrims called it "dissoluteness"—of the Dutch. When they were old enough, some of their children left Leyden to become soldiers and sailors.

The Exodus

It was for sound and sensible reasons, not, Bradford insists, "out of any newfangledness or other such like giddy humor," that the Pilgrims decided upon emigration to America. In 1616, William Brewster was sent to England to procure a grant from the Virginia

Company and to obtain crown permission to establish a colony in English possessions across the Atlantic. In the fall of 1617, John Carver and Robert Cushman conferred with highly placed sympathizers in London.

Through Sir Edwin Sandys the Pilgrims obtained crown permission. King James refused to grant them religious toleration but allowed them to go and indicated that they would not be molested in New England as long as they behaved themselves. When he asked how they expected to support themselves, he was told probably by fishing. "Very good," said the king. "It was the Apostles' own calling."

The Pilgrims then obtained a patent from the Virginia Company and another from Holland in case they decided to settle in the Dutch colony at the mouth of the Hudson River. Through Robert Cushman they made their financial arrangements with Thomas Weston and a London company of some seventy merchants who put up about seven thousand pounds to finance the undertaking.

The terms of the agreement with the London company were that every person aged sixteen or over who sailed as an emigrant would have one share, worth ten pounds, free in the enterprise and a second if he paid his own passage. All of the emigrants would be provided with food, drink, and clothing out of the fund provided by the investors, and all of the profits got by trade, working, fishing, or in any other way would go into this fund. At the end of seven years all capital and profits, houses, lands, goods and chattels would be divided equally between the London investors and the Pilgrims.

The Pilgrims had asked, rather greedily, to have two days off each week for themselves and to keep for themselves the houses they expected to build and the land on which they built them. This was refused.

The larger part of the Leyden congregation voted to remain in Leyden with John Robinson. The emigrating Pilgrims bought a small ship, the *Speedwell,* in Holland and hired a larger ship, the *May-*

The *Mayflower II*, a 104-foot-long replica of the original ship, was presented to Americans as a good will gesture by the British, and sailed from England to America in 1957 with a crew of thirty-three. It is built of Devon oak as the first vessel was

flower, of 180 tons, in England. After an emotional parting, the *Speedwell* sailed from Delfthaven in late July 1620 and at South-ampton joined the *Mayflower* and the rest of the Pilgrims.

The two ships set out, but the *Speedwell* sprang a leak and both ships stopped at Dartmouth so that it could be repaired. About three hundred miles off Land's End the *Speedwell* began to leak again, and both ships went back, this time to Plymouth. About 20 passengers were left ashore. The rest of the Pilgrims, 102 of them, sailed from Plymouth, Devon, in the *Mayflower* on September 6, 1620.

The Voyage

All aboard were not Pilgrims. Some, to distinguish them from the "saints," were "strangers." Miles Standish, who had served in the Lowlands as an English mercenary, was hired as military leader. John

Alden was engaged as a cooper. Other workers were hired, and, though it seems strange now, some Pilgrim families had their servants and a number of families had additional children as wards.

For some days a good wind sped the *Mayflower* westward, yet many of the passengers grew seasick. As often happens, this became a matter of merriment to some of the unafflicted. Like any Puritan of his time, William Bradford saw pious meaning, poetic justice as well as tragedy, in one shipboard incident.

> There was a proud and very profane young man, one of the seamen, of a lusty, able body, which made him the more haughty; he would always be contemning the poor people in their sickness and cursing them daily with grievous execrations; and did not

This cutaway of a typical merchantman of the early 1600s is based on actual plans of the *Mayflower II*. On the main deck, from left: the pilot's cabin, the helmsman, men hoisting the main yard, and sailmenders in the forecastle. On the gun deck, men getting the anchor up by windlass. Below, water and beer casks, ship's stores, galley, and men coiling the anchor line

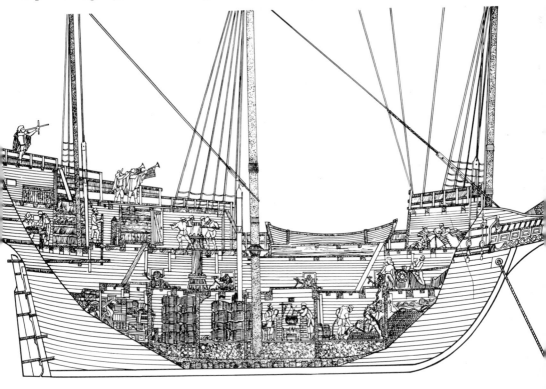

"Clad in doublet and hose, and boots of Cordovan leather . . . short of stature he was, but strongly built and athletic." This is Miles Standish, as depicted by Howard Chandler Christy in Longfellow's *The Courtship of Miles Standish*

let to tell them that he hoped to help cast half of them over-board before they came to their journey's end, and to make merry with what they had, and if he were by any gently reproved, he would curse and swear most bitterly. But it pleased God before they came half seas over to smite this young man with a grievous disease, of which he died in a desperate manner, and so was him-self the first that was thrown overboard.

Storms struck the *Mayflower* in mid-ocean, cracking one of the main beams of the ship. Fortunately one of the passengers had brought "a great iron screw" (evidently a jack) with him from Holland with which the beam was raised and mended. After caulk-ing the leaking seams of the ship, they went on under lessened sail. Only one passenger died, a young man named William Butten, ser-vant to Samuel Fuller.

Landfall at Provincetown

At daybreak November 9, 1620, the *Mayflower* sighted the high-lands of Cape Cod, then sailed south for New Amsterdam at the

Hudson's mouth. Driven back by shoals and breakers, the ship returned to the tip of the Cape. The day before they landed, determined on unity and fearful of disaffection among some who had joined them in England, the Pilgrims drew up the famous Mayflower Compact. Forty-one of them signed the document that is generally regarded as displaying a concept of responsible self-government which was in advance of its time. The original text of the Compact has never been found. This is its text as given in *Mourt's Relation*, which was published in London in 1622.

> In the name of God, Amen. We whose names are underwritten, the loyal subjects of our dread sovereign lord King James, by the grace of God, of Great Britain, France, and Ireland King, Defender of the Faith, etc.
>
> Having undertaken, for the glory of God, and advancement of the Christian faith, and honor of our king and country, a voyage to plant the first colony in the northern parts of Virginia, do by these presents solemnly and mutually in the presence of God and one of another, covenant and combine ourselves together in a civil body politic, for our better ordering and preservation, and furtherance of the ends aforesaid; and by virtue hereof to enact, constitute, and frame such just and equal laws, ordinances, acts, constitutions, offices from time to time, as shall be thought most meet and convenient for the general good of the colony; unto which we promise all due submission and obedience. In witness whereof we have hereunder subscribed our names; Cape Cod, the 11th of November, in the reign of our sovereign lord King James, of England, France and Ireland eighteenth and of Scotland fifty-fourth, Anno Domini 1620.

The shoreline has changed in more than three and a half centuries. The exact spot where the Pilgrims landed after a voyage of sixty-five days is marked now by a mural in the dining room of the Provincetown Inn. They fell upon their knees and blessed God for deliverance from the perils of the deep, stood thankfully on the firm earth. Mingled with their thankfulness were less pleasant emotions. Bradford—whose wife drowned off Provincetown a few days after the landing—tells of them in an eloquent and moving passage.

> . . . they now had no friends to welcome them nor inns to enter-
> tain or refresh their weatherbeaten bodies; nor houses or much
> less towns to repair to, to seek for succour. . . . And for the
> season it was winter, and they that know the winters of that
> country know them to be sharp and violent, and subject to cruel
> and fierce storms. . . . Besides, what could they see but a hideous
> and desolate wilderness, full of wild beasts and wild men. . . . If
> they looked behind them, there was the mighty ocean which
> they had passed and was now as a main bar and gulf to separate
> them from all the civil parts of the world. If it be said they had
> a ship to succour them, it is true, but what heard they daily
> from the master and company? But with what speed they should
> look out a place where they would be, at some near distance; for
> the season was such that he would not stir from thence till a safe
> harbor was discovered by them, where they would be, and he
> might go without danger; and that victuals consumed apace but
> he must and would keep sufficient for themselves and their
> return.

The Pilgrims saw great schools of whales playing in Cape Cod Bay. They could have got thousands of pounds worth of whale oil had they had the equipment to take them. While they were still at Provincetown the first child, Peregrine White, was born to the immigrants in America. He lived to be eighty-four. His will can be seen in Pilgrim Hall in Plymouth alongside the spectacles of Peter Brown. At least one of the *Mayflower's* passengers wore eyeglasses.

Exploration

On the day of the landing fifteen or sixteen well-armed men rowed ashore. They found sand dunes much like those in Holland, but also good black earth, open woods of oak, pine, sassafras, birch, holly, ash, and walnut. They filled their boat with sharp-smelling juniper branches which they burned aboard the *Mayflower*.

On Monday, the thirteenth of November, the Pilgrims unshipped their shallop, a large longboat fitted with sail and oars. The ship's

Typical armor worn by the Pilgrims in 1620 included the steel corselet and sword. Miles Standish's armor-plated army consisted of eight or nine men

carpenter set to work repairing the damage done in stowing it and by people sleeping in it on the voyage over in the crowded ship. The women went ashore to do much needed washing. On the Wednesday a party of sixteen men under Miles Standish, each wearing steel corslet and sword and carrying his musket, went to seek a suitable site for settlement.

They saw a few Indians who fled, camped for the night, came on springs of fresh water in the morning, "of which," says *Mourt's Relation,* "we were heartily glad, and sat us down and drunk our first New England water with as much delight as ever we drank drink in all our lives." They found Indian cornfields of the summer past, then dug up and carried off stored corn which the Indians had buried. They came on other Indian signs. As they examined a sapling bent over a path, William Bradford was caught in a noose of cunningly made rope. It was a deer trap. Promising themselves to pay the unseen Indians for what they had taken, they stored the corn they had found for seed and were picked up by the *Mayflower's* longboat.

Another expedition of thirty-five men under Captain Jones of the *Mayflower* followed Indian paths, dug up Indian graves, and shot three fat geese and six ducks. Near tragedy was averted when

Plymouth Rock has been moved several times since the Pilgrims landed, but today it lies underneath a portico exactly where they stepped ashore. *Mayflower II* floats at anchor adjacent to Plymouth Rock

a boy playing with his father's musket in a *Mayflower* cabin started a fire which almost ignited a half barrel of gunpowder.

When the shallop was finally repaired, ten determined men set out in it to find a place for their permanent settlement. They had their first encounter with the Indians when a shower of arrows fell among them on what is now Eastham beach. They gave this place the name by which it is still known, First Encounter.

Both aboard the Mayflower, where the women and children remained, or exploring in the shallop or ashore, the Pilgrims were wet, cold, and hungry. There were harsh winds and gales of rain. Six inches of snow fell. The men shot an eagle whose flesh, they thought, tasted like mutton. In their shallop they circled the inner shore of the Cape and reached the mainland of Massachusetts searching for what their pilot remembered as a good harbor there. The mast of the shallop snapped in a storm, and its rudder broke, yet they made the shelter of a small island. The next morning they reached shore and landed, according to tradition, on Plymouth Rock. The date by our modern calendar was December 22, 1620.

Founding of Plymouth

The *Mayflower* followed. Because of the shallowness of the water, it anchored about a mile and a quarter off Plymouth Rock on December 16. All of the Pilgrims were at Plymouth now.

Here they found good water, sand, gravel, clay. They found fruit trees—cherry and plum—and herbs. They kept searching for a spot accessible to the sea, for their principal profits would have to come from fishing, and suitable for growing corn. They were short of food, "especially our beer," as *Mourt's Relation* says, when they chose a site where there. was a good spring and which the Indians had planted three of four years before with corn. It was on a commanding hill facing the bay. There they could build a platform on which to install their small cannon.

Neither the Pilgrims nor the Puritans observed Christmas, which they considered a pagan festival. On Monday, December 25, all the men went ashore to fell and saw timber and began to erect the gun platform which later they made their combined fort and house of worship. Daily the men waded ashore through the icy water to work on the building of a common house about twenty feet square and to begin work on a double row of cottages along a single street.

They were continually fearful of Indian attack and puzzled as to why they saw none of the natives. All reports had been that the land was thickly populated. Single men were attached to families so that fewer cottages—nineteen in all—would have to be built. Wisely, their leaders decided that the work would go forward faster if each man built his own house rather than their working in common.

Foul weather, cold, and consequent illness delayed the work. Most of the Pilgrims, used to the milder climate of England or the moist climate of Holland, were sick. One night they trembled to hear what they thought were two lions roaring. Early the morning of January 14, 1621, the thatched roof of their common house, in which men slept side by side in cramped quarters, caught fire from chimney sparks and went up in flames. The roof burned off, but the building's frame stood unharmed.

The *Mayflower,* whose captain had first been so anxious to return to England, delayed sailing. Illness and death had struck the crew of fifty-six as well as those who had been their passengers. Before the *Mayflower* left, she had lost half her company, including several officers, boatswain, cook, gunner, and three quartermasters.

There were a few encouraging signs. The *Mayflower's* captain returned from a fishing trip with three seals and a large cod. Another day one of the sailors found a live herring on the shore. Captain Jones ate it for his supper.

The Pilgrims were not solemn-faced puritanical fanatics in quaint costumes who were intent on becoming figures of legend and romance. Decent, very human people who had emigrated in the hope of bettering themselves spiritually and materially, they were men and women of humble social status—exiled heretics in their second place of exile. They were possessed of great courage and gentle determination, but many were ill equipped physically to endure the rugged winter climate of Massachusetts or to survive the primitive conditions to which their hopes had brought them.

There were no Paul Bunyans, Mike Finks, or Daniel Boones among them. Most had been farmers in England; they had worked indoors in Holland. None of them was young and robust. They were small men. The doughty Miles Standish—"Captaine Shrimpe," Thomas Morton called him a few years later—was five feet two inches tall.

The suffering of these people was intense that first winter. Poor and in debt, they worked to exhaustion. The Sabbath was a day of rest, but they spent it in earnest devotions. Four of the *Mayflower's* passengers were dead before the ship reached Plymouth. Exposure and poor food felled most of the rest with illness. John Carver, whom they had chosen their first governor, was stricken. On January 11, 1621, "William Bradford being at work (for it was a fair day) was vehemently taken with a grief and pain, and so shot to his huckle-bone," the unknown writer of *Mourt's Relation* reported.

Carver recovered from his first illness but died on April 5. Fifty —almost half—of the colony were dead before the summer of 1621. Only twelve of the original twenty-six family heads and four of the twelve single men were still alive. Many of the women were dead. The first Pilgrim child in Plymouth was born dead.

The Indians

The Pilgrims could not know why they saw none of the large numbers of Indians told about by Pring and Smith. In 1617 the Bubonic plague had killed more than half the natives between the Penobscot River and Narragansett Bay. The Massachusetts tribe had been almost wiped out. Many of the surviving Indians believed that the plague had been visited on them because of the murder of some white fishermen in 1616. They thought that the Pilgrims whom they watched from hiding had the power to loose the plague and destroy them. They also feared the Englishmen's guns.

A depiction of the Pilgrims' first Indian visitor, Samoset, who walked alone into the Pilgrims' settlement and remained their ally and friend for many years

It took as much courage as the Pilgrims themselves showed for an Algonquin named Samoset, armed only with a bow and two arrows, one of them unheaded, to walk alone into Plymouth. He greeted them in the broken English he had learned from fishermen in southern Maine, where he was a sagamore. Tall, straight, black-haired, he was a marvel to the Pilgrims who were alarmed at first but eager to know all that Samoset could tell them. Modestly they covered his nakedness with a horseman's coat. They gave him duck meat, biscuit, butter, and cheese, which he relished. When he asked for beer, they gave him brandy instead.

Samoset told them that every one of Plymouth's Indian inhabitants had been killed by the plague. He told them of nearby tribes, their numbers and their leaders. Samoset stayed the night in the house of Stephen Hopkins, the cautious Pilgrims keeping a watch over him. When he left the next day for the Wampanoag village of which Massasoit was chief, they gave him a knife, a bracelet, and a ring.

A few days later Samoset returned with five other tall Indians who, to the Pilgrims, resembled gypsies. They were dressed in deerskins, one with a wild cat's pelt over his arm. All wore leather hose. Their faces were painted. They sang and danced for the English who feasted them, gave them gifts, and asked them to bring furs to trade. The Indians promised to return tools of the Pilgrims which they had stolen in the woods.

When Samoset returned March 22, 1621, he brought Squanto with him as an emissary for his chief, Massasoit. Backed by sixty of his men, Massasoit showed himself in the distance. Edward Winslow was sent to him with gifts of knives, jewels, and liquor. He told the chief that the Pilgrims wished to be friends and to trade with him.

Massasoit kept Winslow as a hostage, putting him in the charge of his brother, Quadequina. Then the chief with twenty of his men walked into the village leaving all their bows and arrows behind him. Standish conducted the chief to one of the houses being built. A rug

The treaty between Governor Carver and
Massasoit was solemnized in Indian fashion.
Today, a bronze statue on Cole's Hill honors
Massasoit, the Wampanoag chief. The bones
of those Pilgrims who died during the first
winter are interred in a sarcophagus on Cole's
Hill also

and cushions were placed on the floor. The governor and the chieftain kissed, ate, and drank brandy.

At this ceremonial meeting Massasoit and the Pilgrims drew up a treaty which neither party ever violated. It was honestly observed for more than fifty years. Its simple terms, as given in *Mourt's Relation*, were these:

1. That neither he nor any of his should injure or do hurt to any of our people.
2. And if any of his did do hurt to any of ours, he should send the offender that we might punish him.
3. That if any of ours were taken away when our people were at work, he should cause them to be returned, and if ours did any harm to any of his, we would do the like to them.
4. If any did unjustly war against him, we would aid him; if any did war against us, he should aid us.
5. He should send to his neighbor confederates, to certify them of this, that they might not wrong us, but might be likewise comprised in the conditions of peace.
6. That when their men came to us, they would leave their bows and arrows behind them, as we should do our pieces when we came to them.

Both Samoset and Squanto, destined to befriend the Pilgrims in many ways for many years, stayed the night this time. The others said that they would soon return to plant their corn and spend the summer just across the brook from the Pilgrims' street of cottages. The next day at noon Squanto went to fish for eels. He trod them from the sand, then caught them in his hands. The Pilgrims found them fat and sweet.

The Pilgrims had seen many deserted Indian dwellings and cornfields. They knew now why they were deserted, and they soon knew more of how the Indians of the Cape and of the Massachusetts shoreline lived.

They were Algonquins, a family which included in New England the Wampanoag, Narragansett, Massachusetts, Penobscot, Pequot, and Abnaki tribes. They lived in large oval huts made by bending saplings and then covering the domed frame with elm or birchbark or, in winter, mats of cattail rushes. They lived on fish, shellfish, and game, particularly deer which they hunted for their skins as well as for meat. In their fields and gardens they grew corn, beans, pumpkins, and squash. From these Indians the Pilgrims learned the many uses of corn in hominy, succotash, and bread. The Indians taught them how to obtain and prepare persimmons, popcorn, and maple sugar. It was Squanto who showed the Pilgrims how to plant a herring for fertilizer in each hill of corn.

The Indian men wore moccasins, leggings, a breechcloth, and, in cold weather, a robe. The women wore skirts of deerskin and sometimes a jacket. Until they were about ten years old Indian children wore nothing. Both men and women treated their hair, always glossy black, with bear fat, sometimes mixing it with soot, but the men outdid the women in the imaginative use of cosmetics. They painted their faces with animal and mineral dyes to suit their fancies. Both

Early bowl and pestle, the Indian method for pounding corn. An ear of popcorn similar to that introduced to the white settlers by the Indians is also shown

men and women carried small bags of dyes mixed with animal fats. The women used fish oil and eagle fat to keep their skin smooth, sometimes adding a red pigment to color their cheeks. They even used black pigment for eye shadow.

The Algonquins believed in one all-powerful god, Manitou (Manabus, Maniboxbo), who remade the world after it had been destroyed by a great flood. Each Indian male of any standing had his totem, his guardian spirit who watched over him always. Thus an Indian was never alone.

Indian doctors used many roots and herbs, remedies which many of the white men came to value. When they were faced with community problems, such as food shortages or epidemics or when they had to make decisions regarding war or peace, the Indians had their own town meetings. They gathered in powwows, eating, drumming, and deliberating about their fires.

To the best of their ability, the Indians, whose way of life had been established for centuries and who had a civilization of their own, tried to be friendly with the usurping colonists. Weakened in numbers by disease and fearful of the white men's firearms, at war with tribal enemies, they acted in part from self-interest. The colonists, even the God-fearing Pilgrims, accepted all they could obtain in trade and friendship but treated the Indians with suspicion. As

The Governor Bradford House at Plimoth Plantation, where visitors may step back over three hundred years in time to see how the Pilgrims lived

well as upon kindness they depended on the natives' fear of Miles Standish and his armed and armor-plated army of eight or nine men.

One kind deed helped ensure the friendship of the Wampanoags. When Massasoit fell seriously ill, one of the leaders of the Plymouth colony, and one of its historians, went to the chief's wigwam and nursed him back to health.

Departures and Arrivals

The *Mayflower* left Plymouth, April 5, 1621, and made a shorter voyage eastward than it had in coming, arriving in England May 6. The colonists felt much alone now, but the coming of spring and more clement weather allowed them to get forward more rapidly with their building. The gun platform was transformed into a stout blockhouse. More houses went up on the single street which led from the hill to the sea.

John Carver had died, and William Bradford was chosen governor in his stead. Aged thirty-one at the time, Bradford became and remained the able leader of his people, serving as governor or, when he pled off, assistant-governor until 1656. Fair and generous, Bradford was the capable secular head of Plymouth, just as Elder Brewster was its spiritual leader.

By the end of the summer the worst was over for the Pilgrims. They were at peace with the Indians. Seven of their homes had been completed. They had cleared some twenty-six acres of land. They had learned to endure the mosquitoes. Guided by Squanto, they had voyaged to Massachusetts Bay and traded for a large quantity of valuable beaver. They had begun to fish successfully for cod and sea bass.

Their small crop had been good. They began to secure their homes for the winter, storing provisions of meal and corn. They had wild turkey, duck, geese, and venison. A year from their first landing they celebrated the famous first Thanksgiving. Edward Winslow described it in a letter of December 11, 1621, to a friend in England.

G. H. Boughton illustrated the tensions with the Indians in his painting "The March of Miles Standish," which was based on an episode of Longfellow's *The Courtship of Miles Standish*. This steel engraving of his work shows Standish to the left of the leading file; both the leading and rear files have seen military service, so they flank the less experienced civilians in the middle. Hobomek, "friend of the white men," led the small army "to quell the sudden revolt of the savage." Longfellow related that the men seemed like "giants" in the mist; the painting may therefore have more literary than historical accuracy since the Pilgrims were really much shorter than the Indians

> Our harvest being gotten in, our Governor sent four men out fowling so we might after a more special manner rejoice together, after we had gathered the fruits of our labours. They four in one day killed so much food as, with a little help beside, served the Company almost a week. At which time, amongst other recreations, we exercised our arms, many of the Indians coming amongst us, and amongst the rest their greatest king, Massasoit with some 90 men, whom for three days we entertained and feasted. And they went out and killed five deer which they brought to the plantation and bestowed on our Governor and upon the Captain and others.

November 9, 1621, a year from the day the *Mayflower* had first sighted the land of New England, a small ship, the *Fortune,* sailed into Plymouth harbor. It brought thirty-five more of the Leyden congregation, among them Robert Cushman, John Adams, and Jonathan Brewster, eldest son of Elder William Brewster. Love and Wrestling Brewster had come with their mother and father in the *Mayflower*.

The Pilgrims were glad of this reinforcement to their community, but somewhat dismayed. The newcomers arrived without provision or so much as a pot or pan among them. Young men had even discarded their coats and cloaks before they boarded at Plymouth in England and had to be supplied with cheap ready-made garments which the London adventurers had sent in the ship. Disapprovingly, Bradford wrote, "most of them were lusty young men, and many of them wild enough, who little considered whither or about what they went. . . ."

It was soon after the arrival of the *Fortune* that Bradford displayed his courage and sagacity in a test case. Canonicus, sachem of the unfriendly Narragansetts, had a messenger toss a bundle of newly

The first settlers of Massachusetts, both Pilgrims and Puritans, had a task before them that demanded much ingenuity and resourcefulness. This is a Puritan housewife operating a strange type of spinning wheel; the picture was drawn in 1681, half a century after Massachusetts Bay Colony was founded

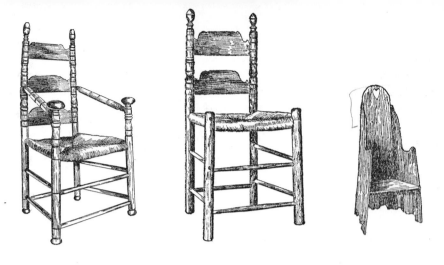

made arrows wrapped in a snakeskin at the door of the governor's house. A friendly Wampanoag confirmed Bradford's opinion that the gesture was a threat and a challenge.

Though the Narragansetts, who had not been decimated by the plague, could muster thousands of warriors and the Pilgrims but about fifty armed men, Bradford stuffed the snakeskin with powder and bullets. He sent it back to Canonicus with a message that if he wanted war he could have it. Canonicus quailed at sight of this symbol of English power and at Bradford's bold statement and desisted.

Manner of Life

When they came to Massachusetts the Pilgrims built cottages of the kind in which they lived in England. The typical house in early Plymouth was of one room built around a huge stone fireplace which served for both heating and cooking. In fact, the fireplace was built first, then the home erected around it. Above the single room was a loft, reached by ladder, in which the children of the family slept. A bed, table, chair, pots and pans, and pewter dishes were the furnishings of the home.

The outsides of the cottages were clapboarded with boards from felled logs sawed in a sawpit. At first roofs were thatched, but so many caught fire that later houses were covered with split cedar

This collection of early Pilgrim chairs includes a Pilgrim slat-back armchair with mushroom posts; a slat-back side chair; a child's wing chair; a roundabout chair with cross stretcher; and a child's high slat-back armchair

shingles. The casement windows of small diamond-shaped panes of glass set in lead were brought intact from England.

Each house had its own small herb garden and usually its wooden fence. The Pilgrims dipped their own candles which at night threw soft light on the unfinished board floors, the stiffly upright chairs, and the Bible on the shelf. Each house had its Bible in a Bible case. The Pilgrims read and studied the Geneva Bible, a version of the Scriptures translated by English Protestants in Geneva. In small type, the Geneva Bible had notes and maps to aid the Puritan reader in study.

The houses of the Pilgrims were tight, snug, and comfortable if unpretentious. There were even a few luxuries, bits of choice china and silver brought from England. Several of the leaders of the colony had fairly extensive libraries. Elder Brewster had what for the time and place was a large collection of religious books. Yet he also had his basket-hilted short sword, for the spiritual leader of the Pilgrims had to go armed like every other man in the colony. Like ordinary men its military leader had to shave. A razor dated 1614 was found at the site of Miles Standish's later house in Duxbury.

Muskets and halberds, breast armor, morions, pikes, and swords were as much a part of life in early Plymouth as cradles and chairs. Many of the Pilgrims' possessions are on display in Pilgrim Hall in

Plymouth, and two and a quarter miles from its original site—now overlaid by downtown Plymouth—is an authentic reproduction of the entire Plimoth Plantation of 1621 to 1627.

The Plymouth Economy

Staying only a few weeks, the *Fortune* set sail for England with a cargo of beaver furs and choice woods. This cargo, worth 500 pounds, was to be Plymouth's first installment on its debt to the London company. Ship and cargo never reached England, for the *Fortune* was seized and despoiled by a French cruiser.

Plymouth prospered slowly and came in time to reach a stable economy, but it never flourished. The friendly Dutch of New Amsterdam sold the Pilgrims wampum and taught them how to use the black and white beads made of shells in trading with the Indians. The Pilgrims traded up and down the coast for furs, grew corn, later raised cattle, but from the viewpoint of the investors the colony was a failure.

In 1624, the London merchants wrote that they had decided to abandon the venture and take their losses rather than spend any more money. They asked the Pilgrims to remit what they could in payment of special debts amounting to 1,400 pounds. They also sent some cattle and commodities for sale to the settlers at a 70 percent markup to cover profits and risks. The risks from shipwreck or piracy were always high.

Miles Standish was sent to London in 1625 to borrow money with which to buy trade goods. He managed to borrow only 150 pounds at 50 percent interest. In 1626, Isaac Allerton, one of the original *Mayflower* passengers and later the colony's inept agent in England, was able to borrow 200 pounds at 30 percent. Interest charges were exorbitant, but the profits in trading with the Indians were correspondingly high.

In 1626, a group of London partners who had bought up the claims of the original London company relinquished all claims to

One of the governors of Plymouth Colony, Edward Winslow in Puritan dress, 1644

the real estate and property of the settlers in consideration of 1,800 pounds to be paid them over a nine-year period. This was the welcome end of the communal scheme in Plymouth. Families now worked for themselves and far more willingly than when the profits from their labors went into a general fund. Each family head was alloted a house, twenty acres of land, and a share of the livestock; one cow and two goats went to every six persons.

In 1633, eight "Undertakers," including Brewster, Winslow, Bradford, Standish, and Alden, took on responsibility for the 1,800 pounds debt in return for a monopoly of the fur trade. They also made themselves responsible for obtaining necessities from England which they would exchange for corn at six shillings a bushel.

The early Pilgrims were not shrewd businessmen. The hard struggle which the Undertakers knew for a time was not made easier by the greediness of one of their London creditors and what was the ineptness, at least, of their own men sent to London as agents, but Plymouth won through.

CHAPTER TWO

The Puritans and Massachusetts Bay Colony

The Puritans who landed in Massachusetts Bay ten years later and some forty miles north of Plymouth were not, like the Pilgrims, an unpretentious people. They had pretentions of many kinds—religious, political, social, and material. They were not a small congregation of humble people seeking from a wilderness and its savage inhabitants asylum they could not find at home. They were a concourse of proud, strong-minded men determined upon pursuing their own way and achieving their own ends.

Defeated in their ambitions in England, the leaders of the emigrating Puritans decided to establish in New England the kind of world in which they wished to live. They would form and govern it by themselves, for themselves, and for nobody else. Many of them were men of influence and affluence in England. They were educated men who had held responsible positions and were used to governing the common people whom they brought with them in large numbers. They were idealistic and earnest in their religious beliefs. They were also hard-headed, hard-fisted, and often hard-hearted. They were self-confident and ambitious. They were well organized, well equipped, strong in purpose and resources. —

English Background

James I, son of Mary Queen of Scots and the first Stuart king of England, ruled not just by blood succession and not at all by consent of the English people, but, he asserted, by divine right. It was

God's will and ordained of heaven that he be king and everyone accept his sovereignty. Well educated, King James adhered to the Church of England both as a workable compromise between Roman Catholicism and Calvinistic Protestantism and because it increased his power.

He showed a certain liberality. The Pilgrims had been forced to flee England under him, but he had allowed their departure for New England. After the suggestion had been made by a Puritan minister and scholar of Oxford, James ordered a translation from "the original tongues" of the Bible which became the Authorized King James Version. Under James, Captain John Smith explored New England. James's son showed no liberality at all.

In the same year, 1625, that he succeeded his father, Charles I married Henrietta Maria, daughter of Henry IV of France. King and court became strongly pro-French, pro-Catholic, and anti-Puritan. Arrogant and arbitrary, Charles I levied heavy taxes on the rising middle class, many of them Puritans, exacted forced loans, and hauled his enemies before the Star Chamber. This secret court conducted by the Privy Council could condemn and sentence without jury trial.

Portrait of King Charles I who with William Laud made life intolerable for the Puritans in England, and thus spurred a great migration to the colonies

Only four years after becoming king, Charles dissolved Parliament, which was Puritan in sympathy, and for eleven years ruled England without it. As far as the Puritans were concerned, Charles I and William Laud, who became in effect his first minister, controlled the country.

President of St. John's College, Oxford, then bishop of Bath and Wells, William Laud was made a Privy Councillor in 1626. He was made chancellor of Oxford in 1630 and finally ecclesiastical head of the Church of England as Archbishop of Canterbury. A bitter opponent of Puritanism and of any semblance of democratic government, Laud was a high churchman, insistent on all the forms and ceremonies of the church, the very signs and symbols which the Puritans most detested. Laud prosecuted and persecuted alike clergymen and lay leaders who deviated from the rules he laid down and made his inquisitorial courts of inquiry as feared as the Star Chamber itself.

This situation made life in England intolerable for many Puritans. They could not worship as they wished; they could not even be sure of retaining their positions, their property, perhaps their freedom. Had the Puritans who came to Massachusetts in 1629 and 1630 remained in England for another ten years, they would have found the situation reversed. By 1640, Parliament was in *de facto* control. Archbishop Laud was beheaded in 1643; Charles I in 1649. Had they waited, the Puritans need never have come to New England, but no more than anyone else could they forsee the future. They knew only that their present status was impossible.

Early Massachusetts Colonies

Colonization in Massachusetts was no longer a new and untried business. The Pilgrims had successfully established themselves in Plymouth. That indefatigable colonizer, Sir Ferdinando Gorges, kept trying. He sent settlers to Maine, but they failed to establish themselves. In 1620, he got the Council for New England established in

Plymouth, Devon, as successor to the northern or Plymouth arm of the Virginia Company. With Gorges as president, the Council obtained all rights to plant, govern, and hold New England as proprietors of the entire North American continent between the fortieth and forty-eighth degrees of latitude. As no one knew the east to west depth of the land, no one bothered about western boundaries to the grant. Considered the founder of Maine, Gorges, in continual dispute with other colonizers he felt infringed on his rights, could not even make good his claims to the territory.

One of the Pilgrim's merchant backers, Thomas Weston, tried to establish a separate colony at Wessagusset (Weymouth) in 1622. Thomas Morton, who so upset both Pilgrims and Puritans, came to New England first with Captain Wollaston in 1622 and established his trading post at Merrymount (Quincy).

The first Puritan colony was set up in Massachusetts when John White, pastor of a congregation of fishermen in Dorchester, England, obtained a grant from the Council for New England, raised three thousand pounds, and sent fourteen men to establish a colony on Cape Ann. This settlement was intended to provide provisions and religious instruction to English fishing crews during the season. This attempt was relinquished after three years, but some of the settlers—among them Roger Conant—went to Naumkeg (Salem) and remained there.

Besides the people in Plymouth and the scattered remnants of these other attempts at colonization there were for half of each year as many as ten thousand Englishmen engaged in the fisheries of Newfoundland. French, Spanish, and English had been fishing off Newfoundland and to the south for over a hundred years.

Massachusetts Bay and Salem Settlement

In 1628, the Council for New England granted Sir Henry Roswell, Sir John Young, Thomas Southcote, John Humfrey, and John Endecott rights running east and west from sea to sea to Massachu-

Woodcut and signature of John Endecott, who headed the Massachusetts Bay Colony in 1628

setts, i.e., all the land from three miles north of the Merrimac River to three miles south of the Charles River.

All the men to whom this grant was made were friends of John White of Dorchester, active proponent of the Puritan cause. Largely through his influence, these men also obtained a royal charter. This gave "The Governor and Company of the Massachusetts Bay in New England" sweeping powers. Investors in the company, called "freemen," could each year forever elect a governor, a deputy-governor, and eighteen assistants. These officials were then empowered to make laws consistent with those of England for their proposed colony, admit new members to the company, and defend the colony against land or sea attack.

John Endecott (it is sometimes spelled "Endicott," but it is "Endecott" on his stone in King's Chapel Burying Ground, Boston) was sent to Salem, Massachusetts, in 1628 as agent of the Massachusetts Bay Company. His instructions from the London merchant who was governor of the Company, Matthew Craddock, were that the teaching of the gospel was to be his first concern.

Three hundred men, eighty women, twenty-six children, forty cows, and forty goats as well as supplies and provisions sailed from the Isle of Wight in six ships about May 1, 1628. Endecott governed the whole, but the spiritual leader of this first contingent of emigrating Puritans was Francis Higginson, a scholar of Emmanuel College, Cambridge. Higginson called the passengers of his ship to its stern for a last sight of England. In his *Magnalia Christi Americana*, Cotton Mather quotes what Higginson said as the ship sailed past Land's End.

> We will not say as the Separatists were wont to say at their leaving of England, Farewell Babylon, farewell Rome! but we will say, farewell dear England! farewell the Church of God in England, and all the Christian friends there! We do not go to New England as Separatists from the Church of England, though we cannot but separate from the corruptions in it, but we go to practice the positive part of church reformation, and propagate the gospel in America.

The Endecott flotilla reached Salem in June and quickly established a community where there had been only a group of fishermen and traders. To protect rights granted by patents and charter, a few were sent to build a nonconformist settlement at what became Charlestown on Massachusetts Bay. When two of his councillors persisted in using the Book of Common Prayer of the Church of England, the dictatorial Endecott—who would become notorious for his narrow-minded and militant Puritanism—deported them back to England. It was a portent.

This was the initial landing of a large number of Puritans in Massachusetts. It might have been the sole expedition, and Salem and Charlestown might have been the only Puritan settlements in a colony approximating the size of Plymouth. Instead this proved to be merely the advance thrust of a great migration.

The Cambridge Compact

Conditions in England did not improve for Puritans remaining there—they worsened. A group of moneyed and influential Puritans, unhappy and alarmed, took to meeting at Tattershall, seat of the Puritan Earl of Lincoln near Boston. They were men of the upper middle class. Some bore titles; many of them were related. John Humfrey and Isaac Johnson were married to daughters of the earl. Thomas Dudley of Northampton had fought for King Henry of Navarre. Thomas Leverett was an alderman of Boston, Lincolnshire. Among the group was Simon Bradstreet, husband of the Puritan poetess Anne Bradstreet. Many of the men were members of the Massachusetts Bay Company, which was holding its meetings in Boston, England.

It was Governor Matthew Craddock who made a discovery. He pointed out that the Company's charter did not say where its meetings had to be held.

The daring idea took hold that the headquarters of the Massachusetts Bay Company could be in New England rather than in old England.

A number of these well-endowed and well-placed Puritan leaders had been thinking about emigrating to escape their troubles and advance their fortunes. More Puritans and their families decided they would emigrate—but all of them would go only if they could take the charter of the Massachusetts Bay Company with them and govern their overseas colony without interference from the authorities in England.

Meeting in Cambridge, where many of them had been to college, twelve men signed an agreement which said in part:

> We will be ready in our persons, and with such of our several families that are to go with us, to embark for the said plantation by the first of March next . . . provided always that before the last of September next the whole government, together with the patent for the said plantation, be first legally transferred.

The men who signed this Cambridge Compact, August 26, 1629, were Sir Richard Saltonstall, Thomas Dudley, Richard Vassall, Nicholas West, Kellam Browne, Isaac Johnson, John Humfrey, John Sharpe, Increase Nowell, William Pynchon, William Colborn, and John Winthrop.

At a meeting in London, August 28, the General Court of the Company were made "assistants." Humfrey was made deputy-governor, with Thomas Dudley serving in his place when Humfrey's departure from England was delayed. John Winthrop was elected governor. For the first time an English colony in New England would be self-governing. It would be responsible to no company in England and only nominally responsible to England itself.

John Winthrop and the Great Migration

John Winthrop's paternal grandfather, Adam Winthrop, left the family farm, became a master clothier in London, made a fortune, and at the early age of forty-five retired. He bought Groton Manor at Edwardston in Suffolk, which had belonged to the Abbey of Bury St. Edmunds. He became a country gentleman, a squire, a magistrate, gentleman of the village, with the presentation of the living of Groton church one of his prerogatives. His son, another Adam Winthrop, succeeded his father as lord of the manor. He managed his estates, practiced law in London, and became auditor of Trinity College, Cambridge.

Behind John Winthrop, then, were two generations of power and influence. John Winthrop attended Trinity College for about two years, married the first of his four wives when he was only seventeen, then followed his father's legal profession, beginning to serve as a

John Winthrop, leader of the great Puritan migration to America who became governor of the Massachusetts Bay Colony in 1630

magistrate when he was only eighteen. A more serious Puritan than his father and grandfather had been, he prospered in London, becoming an attorney of the Court of Wards and Liveries. Part of his responsibility was to draft bills for Parliament.

A scholar and a gentleman, John Winthrop was a man of standing and repute. As a Puritan, he stood in opposition to the church policies of Charles I and the rule of Bishop Laud. He was thus one of the many men of wealth and position whose Puritan principles stood between them and preferment in the government.

When he closed Parliament in 1629 and had its Puritan leaders imprisoned, Charles I closed the possibility of a Parliamentary career to John Winthrop. Married for the third time, with many children and even grandchildren, Winthrop was forty-two years old when he became governor of the Massachusetts Bay Company. His compelling motive for emigration was religious. Of the projected colony in Massachusetts he said, "God hath provided this place to be a refuge for many whome he means to save out of the generall calamity, seeing the church hath noe place to flie into but the wilderness, what better work can there be, than to goe & provide tabernacle and foode for her against she comes thether." His second motive may well have been ambition. He hoped to realize in New England that of which he felt thwarted in England. "If he should refuse this opportunitye, that talent which God hath bestowed upon him for publike service were like to be buried." A third motive Winthrop shared with his fellows. They were men of large affairs, businessmen who hoped to reap profit from their emigration.

The Puritans organized their large undertaking efficiently and carefully. Sixteen ships were readied to carry about one thousand people, their provisions, equipment, trading goods, and cattle across the North Atlantic. Gentlemen and their families, yeomen farmers, tradesmen, mechanics, and stockholders of the Company were among the passengers. This was a large-scale operation which in the end cost nearly 200,000 pounds—perhaps forty to fifty million United States dollars in the 1960s.

The *Arbella,* a reproduction of the flagship that brought Governor Winthrop with the Massachusetts Bay charter to Salem in 1630

Some ships of the Puritan fleet sailed from Bristol and Plymouth. The Rev. John Cotton, pastor of St. Bodolph's Church in Boston and the leading Puritan divine in England, preached a farewell sermon to those from the east of England who left Southampton in four ships on March 26, 1630. Aboard the *Arbella*—named for the Lady Arbella, sister of the Earl of Lincoln and wife of Isaac Johnson, who was aboard with her husband—were also John Winthrop, Sir Richard Saltonstall, Simon Bradstreet, Thomas Dudley, William Coddington, and the minister George Phillips.

It was a long but not unpleasant voyage across the Atlantic. The *Arbella* was usually in sight and sound of her three sister ships. Messages passed back and forth. Boys romped and played games with the seamen. Their elders planned ahead and conducted services of worship. Responsible for the entire enterprise, John Winthrop recorded the events of each day in his diary. John Winthrop's *Journal*, later titled *The History of New England* is the invaluable record of Massachusetts Bay, just as *Mourt's Relation* and Bradford's *Of Plymouth Plantation* are of the Pilgrim's earlier-founded colony.

Aboard ship, Winthrop heard complaints and tried to correct unpleasant conditions. One complaint, at least, showed that, Puritans or no, some travelers of 1630 were not too different from some today. The *Arbella* had not been long at sea when Winthrop recorded, "This day our captain told me, that our landmen were very nasty and slovenly, and that the gundeck, where they lodged, was so beastly and noisome with their victuals and beastliness as would much endanger the health of the ship." Winthrop had the gundeck cleaned and ordered better behavior.

Aboard ship, Winthrop also composed a statement of the situation and intent of the emigrating Puritans. Nobility and clarity mingle in these words from "A Modell of Christian Charity."

> Thus stands the case between God and us. We are entered into a Covenant with Him for this work. We have taken out a commission. The Lord has given us leave to draw our own articles. . . . For this end we must knit together in this work, as one man. We must entertain each other in brotherly affection. We must be willing to abridge ourselves of our superfluities for the supply of others' necessities. We must uphold a familiar commerce together in all meekness, gentleness, patience, and liberality. We must delight in each other; make other's condition our own, rejoice together, mourn together, labor and suffer together, always having before our eyes our commission and community in the work, as members of the same body. . . .

Puritan Settlements

After a voyage of seventy-six days the *Arbella* reached Salem on June 22, 1630. Endecott welcomed the new governor and his staff at dinner that night with "a good venison pasty and good beer."

Seaworn voyagers went ashore and picked strawberries on Cape Ann.

Eighty of the Salem colony had died during the winter. Stores were low. It was too late in the year for the newcomers to plant a crop for harvesting in the fall, and there would be many to feed. Seven or eight hundred people came with Winthrop. As the other ships of the Puritan fleet landed, there were soon a thousand new settlers.

Immediately John Winthrop set about finding "a place for our sitting down." As his son, another John Winthrop, who was to become governor of Connecticut, wrote years later, there was "everything to doe as in the beginninge of the world."

The Puritans did not settle in one small community. There were many of them. They had considerable resources, and their charter gave them the rights to a large territory. Salem and Charlestown on Boston harbor already existed. Settlements were quickly established at Lynn, Dorchester, and Medford. Sir Richard Saltonstall and the Rev. George Philips settled in Watertown. The strong-minded Thomas Dudley, who had been trained in the household of the Earl of Northampton, began building a mile below them on the Charles. William Pynchon founded Roxbury, then called Agawam, meaning "place of the river."

Winthrop chose Charlestown, where a house had already been built, as headquarters for the governor and his assistants and began building a home there. Ordinary people who had come with him threw up wigwams, sailcloth tents, and other temporary shelters.

The Puritans had left home as avowed adherents of the Church of England who wished only to cleanse it of what they considered its faults. Yet little more than a month after their first landing they declared their religious independence. In effect, they became Separatists when Winthrop, Dudley, Isaac Johnson, and John Wilson signed the Church Covenant. This united the New England Puritans in one congregation which became the First Church of Boston.

The first Court of Assistants this side of the Atlantic was held in Charlestown, August 23, 1630. The Puritans had come to Massachusetts to found a Bible Commonwealth. Thus it was natural that the first decree of the court was that houses should be erected for the ministers of the various plantations at public expense.

The new settlement in Charlestown was soon in distress. Insufficient food of the kind to which the English were accustomed contributed to widespread illness which resulted too often in death. The Lady Arbella died; saintly Isaac Johnson died. The Company's physician, Dr. William Gager, and the Rev. Francis Higginson of Salem died. Edward Johnson, who was one of the survivors, described this unhappy time in his *Wonder-Working Providence.*

> . . . almost in every family, lamentation, mourning, and woe was heard, and no fresh food to cherish them. It would assuredly have moved the most lockt-up affections to teares, no doubt, had they past from one hut to another, and beheld the piteous case these people were in. And that which added to their present distresse was the want of fresh water; for although the place did afford plenty, yet for the present they could find but one springe, and that not to be come at but when the tide was downe.

Founding of Boston

It was at this crucial juncture that William Blackstone called on Governor Winthrop. A graduate of Emmanuel College, Cambridge, and a clergyman of the Church of England, Blackstone had come to Massachusetts with Gorge's expedition in 1623. Fond of his books (he had 180 of them) and of his garden, he lived as a recluse on the Shawmut peninsula opposite the mouth of the Charles River. There was a good spring there on what was called Trimount or Trimontaine. Blackstone invited the Puritans to join him there, and they accepted.

Winthrop had the frame of the house he was building in Charlestown moved to the new location, across part of Massachusetts Bay to the south, on this peninsula that was almost an island. The ground was clear. The configuration of the land made it comparatively safe from Indian attack. John Smith had located a Boston on his map of 1614, but the Puritans named this spot on their own. The Lady Arbella and Isaac Johnson had come from Boston in England. The Rev. John Cotton had his church there. On September 17, 1630, the Court of Assistants, Governor Winthrop presiding, passed a resolution "That Trimontaine shall be called Boston." In November, Winthrop dated a letter to his wife, Margaret, who had remained in England to see to the disposition of their estates, from "Boston in Mattachusetts [sic]."

Thus Boston became the capital of Massachusetts Bay, and William Blackstone lost his home. In desperate straits, the Puritans had been glad to accept his proffered hospitality, but they could not long countenance a regular Church of England clergyman among them, and William Blackstone could not long endure the Puritans. In 1634 he moved to Rhode Island, remarking that he had left England because he did not like the lord-bishops and he would not now be subject to the lord-brethren.

The Government and the Church

As many have pointed out, the Massachusetts Bay Company, which had been organized as a trading company, resembled any business organization. The governor was the president of the corporation, the deputy-governor the executive vice-president. The eighteen assistants were the board of directors. The investors or stockholders —the freemen—were the General Court which met quarterly to elect company officers and to pass on company affairs.

When the Company removed itself to Massachusetts, it transformed itself, as its leaders had planned, into a colony and its officers into the government of the colony. By liberal and often illegal interpretation of its charter, Massachusetts Bay became a Puritan commonwealth which functioned very nearly as an independent state.

It was no democracy. Democracy was not an admired form of government in the seventeenth century. No thinking man wanted rule by the mob. There were the leaders and the led, and both thought this the natural order of things.

English squires and magistrates were accustomed to governing their people, and the farmers and villagers were accustomed to being governed by them. With their charter and Company officers, the Puritans brought with them almost intact the society to which all of them were used. There was, in addition, a sound financial reason for the maintenance of oligarchical control—the freemen had put up the money for the venture. As stockholders, they could not risk interference by uniformed outsiders.

Governor of the colony for nine years, deputy-governor for ten more, always the leader in Massachusetts Bay, John Winthrop considered democracy the worst of all possible forms of government. Thomas Dudley, who almost alternated in office with Winthrop, was less liberal, an autocrat by training and temperament, a foe of democracy. The Rev. John Cotton, who came to Boston in 1633 to become the powerful religious leaders of Massachusetts Bay, was outspoken in his condemnation. Writing Lord Say in 1636 he said, "Democracy, I do not conceive that ever God did ordayne as a fitt Government, eyther for Church or Commonwealth. If the people be governors, who shall be governed?"

Yet Massachusetts is generally considered to have instituted the kind of essentially democratic government which strongly influenced the republic formed by the thirteen original states of the United States. What happened was that the demands of the people brought about modifications. Willingly or unwillingly the oligarchy which first ruled in Massachusetts had to make concessions.

The change began early. In 1630, the very year of their arrival, a hundred men of the new community demanded to be made freemen. Wisely recognizing the need for more liberality in government, Winthrop concurred. By vote of the General Court, these men were admitted as freemen, with a vote in the management of the colony, in the spring of 1631.

At the same time, the Court ruled that only church members could become freemen of Massachusetts Bay. Most of the rapidly increasing population of the colony were not members of the church, and it was not easy to become a member. The church was as aristocratic as the state. A supplicant for membership had not only to subscribe to all the tenets of Puritan belief, but had also to supply convincing evidence that he had undergone conversion—an emotional experience in which, moved by strong religious feeling (called "affections" then), he became convinced of a new life in the spirit of Christ. The ministers decided whether or not the evidence submitted in open confession entitled the supplicant to become a church member and a "visible saint." The power of the church in the lay affairs of the colony was thus almost absolute.

Thus admitted to church membership, new freemen were entitled to sit with the assistants in the General Court and to vote for governor, deputy-governor, and the other officers. At first the leaders thought and the church agreed that those chosen should hold office

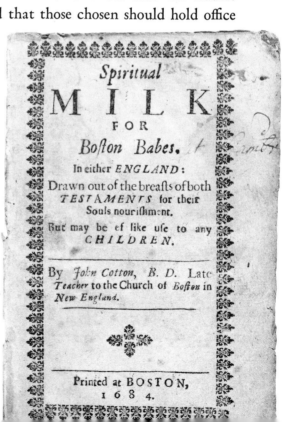

This is the title page of *Spiritual Milk for Boston Babes* by John Cotton, ardent spiritual father of the Massachusetts Bay Colony. Printed in Boston, 1684, it was the first book of any kind written and printed in America for children

for life. The charters and the will of the people changed this to annual elections. The General Court became, essentially, the legislature. The eighteen assistants were the senate or upper house; deputies sent by freemen in other townships to represent them in Boston became the lower house.

Massachusetts in the seventeenth century was a theocracy, a state governed by its church. Ministers were not actually political leaders or magistrates, but a great deal of the real power lay in their hands, and determined ministers, such as John Cotton, made certain that it remained there. Massachusetts had been deliberately founded as a Bible commonwealth, a New Jerusalem, a second Canaan. Even those who were not church members were Puritan in sympathy and reverenced the clergy.

By virtue of their profession, supported by the state, consulted by its leaders, looked to with awe by the common people, the ministers were the chief advisers and confidants of the magistrates. They were the official interpreters of the word of God as laid down in the Bible. They had almost inquisitorial powers to regulate the morals and conduct, public and private, of all the people.

John Cotton

Dean of Emmanuel College as well as rector of St. Bodolph's, John Cotton fled prosecution in England and landed, September 1633, in Boston with his wife and a son born at sea, hence christened Seaborn. Within a month he was made teacher of the Boston church. From that point he was the religious head of Massachusetts Bay. In the theocracy, John Cotton's word was literally law. It is said that whatever he preached soon became actual law or church practice.

Cotton adhered to the Mosaic severity of the Old Testament. He strongly upheld the rights of the magistrates and the right of the church to punish—even by death—those convicted of not conforming to the beliefs and practices of the Massachusetts church. Like many who had been rebellious nonconformists in England, Cotton became the most rigid and intolerant of conformists in New England.

Cotton is described as having been of gentle nature, but the gentleness hardly shows in his insistence on the dominant role of the church, the autocracy of the state, and his proscription of anything approaching liberality. He was active in the persecution and punishment of religious offenders and sharp in religious controversy. These disputes were rife in early Massachusetts, and Cotton took a leading part in them, always on the side of despotic intolerance.

Winthrop's *Journal* ≽

A just and capable administrator, Winthrop was likewise a careful and accurate recorder of events, major and trivial, in Massachusetts Bay. His detailed account is factual and revealing. He recorded the weather, the arrivals of ships, sometimes several at a time—between twenty and twenty-five thousand people came between 1630 and 1640—bringing more Puritans, more cattle, more provisions to Boston.

Dispassionately, Winthrop refers to himself always in the third person. His fairness shows his aristocratic attitude, his decency—and the bigotry and superstitiousness which he shared with the best as well as the worst men of his time. He saw signs and portents of God's intervention or of the devil's machinations everywhere. He wrote of fires, drownings, adultery, quarrels, executions, banishments, and of political and theological disputes. He told of the founding of new Massachusetts settlements, the establishment of new churches, and of relations, sometimes friendly but sometimes strained, with simpler Plymouth.

Winthrop could be explicit in giving the details of barbarous punishments. He could also be movingly restrained. An early entry, Friday, July 2, 1630, reads only: "My son, Henry Winthrop, was drowned at Salem."

Simply as one item in the day's news he wrote in June 1631, ". . . one Philip Ratcliffe, a servant of Mr. Cradock, being convict

. . . of most foul, scandalous invectives against our church and government, was censured to be whipped, lose his ears, and be banished from the plantation, which was presently executed." Humanitarianism was not a characteristic of the seventeenth century anywhere.

In July 1632, Winthrop reported a wonder. "At Watertown there was (in the view of divers witnesses) a great conflict between a mouse and a snake; and, after a long fight, the mouse prevailed and killed the snake. The pastor of Boston, a very sincere, holy man, hearing of it, gave this interpretation; That the snake was the devil, the mouse was a poor, contemptible people, which God had brought hither, which should overcome Satan here, and disposses him of his kingdom." John Winthrop was as credulous as his peers in Europe or America.

He saw a mishap close to him in this light. "Two little girls of the governor's family were sitting under a great heap of logs, plucking of birds, and the wind driving the feathers into the house, the governor's wife caused them to remove away. They were no sooner gone, but the whole heap of logs fell down in the place, and had crushed them to death, if the Lord, in his special providence, had not delivered them."

By 1633, Winthrop was complaining of a scarcity of servants. Too few were coming out from disturbed England. A similar scarcity of workmen had resulted in exorbitant wages. Carpenters were demanding three shillings a day and common laborers two shillings and sixpence. As a result, prices were rising on everything, sometimes to double what they were in England.

Many times John Winthrop noted thankfully, without conscious humor or invidious distinctions, that a ship arrived without loss of a single passenger—except a child or two, or once the ship's carpenter who fell overboard while he was caulking the sides. In 1633, one Robert Cole, a habitual drunkard, was sentenced to wear a red letter "D" around his neck for a year. In 1639, Winthrop noted "the first printing house begun at Cambridge by one Daye." This was Stephen Daye, and the first productions of his press were copies of the freeman's oath, an almanac, and the famous *Bay Psalm Book*.

Winthrop recounted another miracle. His son, already a magistrate in the colony, unwisely stored a thousand books in a room where corn was also stored. Mice ate every page of the Book of Common Prayer but did not touch a leaf of the Psalms or the Greek Testament bound in the same volume or any of the other 999 books. Even Puritan mice detested the English Book of Common Prayer!

Historian as well as dominant Puritan minister of his time, Cotton Mather gives a pleasant sidelight on the character of John Winthrop in his *Magnalia Christi Americana*, which was published in London in 1702.

> And there was one passage of his charity that was perhaps a little unusual; in an hard and long winter, when wood was very scarce at Boston, a man gave him a private information that a needy person in the neighborhood stole wood sometimes from *his* pile; whereupon the governour in a seeming anger did reply, "Does he so; I'll take a course with him; go call that man to me; I'll warrant you I'll cure him of stealing." When the man came, the governour considering that if he had stolen, it was more out of necessity than disposition, said unto him, "Friend, it is a severe winter, and I doubt you are but meanly provided for wood; wherefore I would have you supply yourself at my wood-pile till the cold season be over." And then he merrily asked his friends, "Whether he had not effectually cured this man of stealing his wood?"

CHAPTER THREE

Crime and Punishment

It has sometimes been popular to point to colonial Massachusetts as severe in its laws and barbarous in its punishments. In comparison to England, most of the other countries of Europe, and to some of the other American colonies, Massachusetts was lenient.

In seventeenth-century England murder, manslaughter, heresy, treason, arson, robbery, and all theft where the value of what was stolen was under one shilling were punishable by death. As late as the year 1800, there were 200 capital offenses in England, and men and women were publicly hanged for them.

The object of punishment was to rid society of those who injured it and were a threat to its peaceful existence. Execution was considered the surest method of achieving this end. Banishment was another. It was practiced in ancient Rome. Russia sent its offenders to Siberia. With the founding of its American colonies, England began to substitute transportation to them for execution in some capital cases. It used the colonies as a dumping ground for criminals until after the American Revolution when Australia became its convict camp.

People in the seventeenth and eighteenth centuries did not hesitate to inflict pain. There was a callousness to the suffering of others. Men were burned at the stake in Europe as they had been broken on the wheel. Criminals were maimed and mutilated. This was not just by way of punishment. Before the time of organized police forces,

Pioneer Village, a reproduction of the Salem community of 1630, features the whipping posts, stocks and pillory for which the Puritans became notorious

photographs, and fingerprints, this was to insure identification. People could recognize criminals and beware.

When colonial Massachusetts hanged, branded, whipped or banished, it simply followed what were considered civilized customs of the time. European countries tortured and killed men and women for religious beliefs which differed from those established by law. The way Massachusetts differed was in its attempt to enforce conformity to one religious idea and to regulate human conduct down to the details of dress and speech. Puritan fanaticism shows here, as it shows in the peculiar Puritan idea of punishment. It held lesser offenders up to public ridicule and humiliation in the pillory and the stocks. Possibly the authorities believed in the curative properties of such methods. Certainly it was cruel and unusual punishment. —

Roger Williams

In his diary, January 9, 1631, John Winthrop noted the arrival in Boston of a young man of twenty-seven who had been trained in the law as well as in the church. He described Roger Williams as a "godly minister." Less than five years later Williams was deported as one of the most ungodly men in Massachusetts.

Minister of the church in Salem, Roger Williams enunciated dangerous beliefs. He called for more democratic church rule and for separation of church and state. He advocated religious toleration. Worse, he said the land really belonged to the Indians. October 9, 1635, the General Court found him guilty of spreading "newe and dangerous opinions against the authoritie of the magistrates" and banished him from Massachusetts Bay. When he persisted in his liberal ways, the Court ordered his arrest and return to England but, as Williams wrote years later, "It pleased the Most High to divert my steps into this Bay Narragansett, by the loving private advice of the ever-honored soul, Mr. John Winthrop." In the Spring of 1636, Roger Williams founded a settlement in Rhode Island.

Roger Williams at the council of Canonicus. Respected by the Narragansetts, Williams was later to serve as a mediator between them and the Massachusetts colony. Upon Rhode Island's centenary celebration in 1936, the Massachusetts legislature voted to pardon Williams and revoke the original order of banishment

Anne Hutchinson

Forty-three years old, mother of fourteen, Anne Hutchinson came to Boston in 1634. Vital, vigorous, well-educated, a follower of John Cotton, she began to hold meetings in her home where Boston women discussed the sermons they had heard the previous Sunday. Then she began to preach that the true believer reaches God through the spirit of God dwelling in him rather than through obedience to the laws of the church as expounded by its ministers and enforced by the civil authorities.

This was heresy. Mrs. Hutchinson, who had attracted a large following, was arrested and brought to trial for "traducing the ministers and their ministries." Feeling ran high for and against Anne Hutchinson. Less concerned with the theological implications of her teaching than with its damaging practical effect on the civil authority, John Winthrop sided against her. Ministers worked to reconvert the woman whose teachings threatened to disrupt the colony. They were unsuccessful. After a long and involved trial Anne Hutchinson was cast out of the church and her soul given up to the devil. With her family she emigrated to Rhode Island, and after their removal to New York in 1643 she and all but one of them were massacred by Indians at what is now Pelham Bay.

Thomas Morton of Merry Mount

Nathaniel Hawthorne's "The Maypole of Merry Mount" has made the story of this gentleman amusingly familiar to most. Probably a lawyer, Morton came to Massachusetts with Thomas Weston in 1622 and became a hunter, fisherman, and trader. No Puritan, Morton tried to bring some of the merriment of Merry England to Massachusetts. In 1628 he erected a maypole, and he and his companions and their Indian friends danced and drank around it. The horrified Pilgrims sent Captain Miles Standish and his soldiers to chop it down. Undeterred, the villain—who had all of Hawthorne's sympathy—put up another and taller maypole the next year. This time

John Endecott and his men chopped it down, burned Morton's house, confiscated all his goods, and deported him to England. When, unwisely, he came back and ventured into Boston, he was jailed for a year.

The Quakers

Massachusetts treatment of Quakers was barbarous, but the Quakers did their best to incite it. The Quakers believed in complete separation of church and state. They did not distinguish between clergy and laity. They refused to take oaths of allegiance or perform military service. They did not believe in original sin, the resurrection of the body, or in the efficacy of baptism. What the Puritans held most sacred they condemned—and, as they had done throughout Europe, they condemned it loudly and wildly.

They defiled the Puritan Sabbath. They burst naked or with blackened faces into packed meetings houses. Two women Quakers ran naked through the streets of Boston. A bottle in each hand, one Thomas Newhouse thrust his way into the Old South Meeting House, smashed his bottles together, and cried out to the startled congregation, "Thus will the Lord break you all in pieces!"

Exasperated beyond endurance, Massachusetts banished the Quakers. If they returned, they would be whipped. If they persisted in coming back, they would have their ears cut off and their tongues bored with a hot iron. The death penalty was exacted for extreme offenders. Stern as he was, even John Endecott begged the Quakers to stay away, saying he had no wish for their deaths. Hysterically intent on martyrdom, four of the Quakers—William Robinson, Marmaduke Stevenson, Mary Dyer, and William Leddra—were eventually hanged on Boston Common.

Colonial Massachusetts has often been castigated for the summary dismissal of Roger Williams and Anne Hutchinson and for its brutal treatment of the Quakers. The condemnation is not wholly deserved. Any society—and it is not a society unless it tries to adhere to certain distinctive standards—tries to protect itself against what it sees as dangerous ideas or dangerous people. In early Massachusetts Bay, the religious and the political were one. A threat to the church was a threat to the state itself. Theological differences were as important to the people of the time and place as a television series or professional sports are to contemporary Americans. Heresy was a fact in Massachusetts. It was untrue and repugnant doctrine which could lead to distress in this life and damnation in the next; and the Puritans saw life to come as even more important than this life. Anything which threatened it or the individual soul was evil and had to be stamped out.

At the same time the leaders saw anything or anybody that threatened to undermine the authority of the state as equally dangerous. Like heresy, anarchy and treason had to be scotched.

A Kingdom Apart

Massachusetts Bay dealt summarily with what it considered the enemy within. It was as unyielding and as belligerent with the enemy without, whether that enemy was the Indians, another colony close

To the Puritan way of thinking, theological crimes called for brutal punishment. Quakers, both men and women, were mercilessly scourged, yet many of them pressed the Puritans for even worse punishments

at hand, or England, three thousand miles and six or seven weeks of stormy ocean away.

In the eyes of English authority, Massachusetts showed too great a spirit of independence. It had separated from the Church of England. Its governors and magistrates had arbitrarily assumed authority not granted in the charter. Daily, Massachusetts was drawing educated men and women of intelligence, people of property but Puritan in sympathy, from England. Boston was a busy port engaged in profitable maritime trade. Massachusetts was growing rapidly, not as a colonial dependent and a source of profit to Great Britain but as a self-sufficing community. In 1634, England demanded that Massachusetts return its charter.

Instead of complying with England's demands, John Winthrop ordered out the Massachusetts militia. He had the beacon above the common erected to warn of approaching British naval vessels. He mounted cannon around Boston harbor to resist any invasion by England of what was legally one of her possessions. Though the sympathy of the Massachusetts Puritans was naturally with Cromwell and his forces when the civil war broke out in England, Winthrop kept the colony neutral in act.

John Winthrop and his peers held the Holy Commonwealth of Massachusetts Bay a kingdom apart.

The Laws

The severity of the laws in early Massachusetts is often emphasized. Actually, they were in many instances less severe than those in some of the other colonies, and though the death penalty was on the statute books for a number of offenses, it was sparingly enforced.

In colonial Massachusetts the death penalty could be exacted for idolatry, witchcraft, blasphemy, murder, adultery, abnormal sexual practices, bearing false witness in a capital case, kidnapping, and treason. Some crimes were made capital mostly so that plaintiffs would be careful in making accusations.

64

Massachusetts Bay made church attendance compulsory and levied fines for failure to attend. Whether or not he was a church member, each one was taxed for the support of the clergy. Every town had its whipping post, stocks, and pillory. Offenders were held up to public scorn rather than jailed out of sight.

Swearing was punishable by a fine of ten shillings or humiliation in the stocks. There were laws against smoking in public, then against smoking in private, but they could not be enforced. Most people smoked. In 1634, the General Court passed laws forbidding all lace or silver or gold thread on clothing. Ruffs, beaver hats, and embroidery or needlework on women's caps were forbidden. No one was permitted to wear gold or silver belts or hatbands. Men's coats might have one slit in back and one slit at each cuff, but no more. These slits were designed to show the brightly colored fabrics beneath the coat. Evidently the Puritans showed a regrettable tendency to vanity and ordinary people tended to ape their betters in display. Both inclinations were sinful.

Josselyn's List

An English traveler, John Josselyn visited Massachusetts Bay in 1638, when he called on John Cotton and Governor Winthrop. Twenty-four years later he returned and stayed for seven years. In his *New England's Rarities* he listed some of the Massachusetts laws.

> For being drunk, they either whip or impose a fine of five shillings; so for swearing and cursing, or boring through the tongue with a hot iron.
> For kissing a woman in the street, even though in way of civil salute, whipping or a fine. . . .
> Scolds they gag and set them at their doors, for certain hours, for all comers and goers by to gaze at.
> Stealing is punished with restoring fourfold, if able; if not, they are sold for some years, and so are poor debtors.

The law was no respecter of persons. John Endecott, who enforced them and his own will so vigorously, was called to account in 1632, when he was deputy-governor, for selling seven and a half bushels of corn for ten that he would get after the buyer harvested his crop. In this same year, another man was whipped and branded on the cheeks for selling arms to an Indian. In 1640, a man was banished, on pain of death if he returned, for declaring that he was free from original sin.

At least one law which Massachusetts Bay enacted in 1646 would be applauded today. Any person talking before a court for more than one hour would be fined twenty shillings for each additional hour.

Corporal Punishment

Whipping, branding, cropping of ears, and other forms of corporal punishment were common practice. Massachusetts records cite the punishment meted out to two Quakers.

> . . . they shall by the Constable of Boston, be forthwith taken out of the prison & stript from the Girdle upward by the executioner & tyed to the Carts Tayle & whipt through the Towne with twenty stripes, & then Carried to Roxbury and delivered to the Constable there, who is also to tye them or cause them in like manner to be tyed to a Carts tayle & againe whip them thro' the Towne with tenn stripes, & then Carried to Dedham & delivered to the Constable there . . . & from thence they are immediately to depart this jurisdiction at theire perrill.

Massachusetts sometimes went out of the way to enforce the law, even in places where it lacked authority. In 1634, a trader named Hocking tried to interfere with the trading rights of the Plymouth men in Maine. In a struggle, Hocking killed one of the Pilgrim's agents, whereupon one of them killed Hocking.

Merely because he happened to have been at the scene, Massachusetts arrested John Alden, by this time a Plymouth magistrate, when he went to Boston. When Miles Standish went there with an order for his release, Alden was freed, but Standish was ordered to appear before the next session of the General Court to defend Plymouth's patent to Maine trading. Edward Winslow and William Bradford had to go to Boston to confer with John Winthrop before the matter was settled. Plymouth resented the Bay Colony's high-handed conduct in a case which was not its concern.

Rights Under Law

Laws, of course, are not entirely concerned with crime and punishment. As they do today, these attract attention because of their sensational news value. Life in colonial Massachusetts was strict, and it was regulated—though hardly to the extent that the life of the individual is regulated in the United States today—but most laws were on the books in order to protect the ordinary man and woman in their day-to-day existence.

The men of Plymouth had basically the same characteristics and habits as the men of Massachusetts Bay. They shared the same religious principles, had about the same scruples, ideals, and superstitions. The difference lay mostly in the superior education and wealth of the Bay colony. Plymouth was the scene of one gruesome execution of a teen-age boy for abnormal sexual practices, but it also had its legal guarantees of human rights and freedom. Like Massachusetts Bay, Plymouth based these rights on English common law.

In 1636, Plymouth drew up and established its General Fundamentals, the equivalent of a Bill of Rights. Among other things these fundamentals provided that everyone had a right to equal and impartial justice; everyone had a right to trial by jury; no one could be found guilty of any crime without the evidence of at least two witnesses or adequate circumstantial evidence; no laws could be passed or taxes levied except by consent of the freemen or their assembled representatives.

During the whole of its existence as an independent colony, Plymouth had only five murders. It was not illegal to drink in Plymouth, but it was illegal to get drunk, and fines mounted with the number

MANHOOD

His Children next engage his love and care.

The New England colonists were greatly interested in providing educational books for their children. This is one of a series of watercolors in an unpublished picture book entitled *The Ages of Man,* which was done about 1760 for a child, Freelove Wheeler

of offenses. The Pilgrims' definition of drunkenness was stated in the law. "By drunkedness it is to be understood one that lisps or falters in his speech by reason of overmuch drink, or that staggers in his going, or that vomits."

One thing that neither Massachusetts Bay nor Plymouth would tolerate was play of any kind or working on the Sabbath. One man was severely whipped in Plymouth in 1638 for being caught for the second time working on Sunday.

Laws Concerning Education

Massachusetts is generally credited, and with sufficient reason, with having established free public education in this country. The leading men of Massachusetts Bay were well educated. They valued learning and very early in the history of the colony took steps to ensure its establishment in New England. They had two particular concerns.

One was to found a seat of learning for the education of its ministers. The other was to make sure that people could read their Bibles. In Massachusetts, where the idea can still be discerned, learning was considered to be of God and ignorance of the devil.

The Boston Latin School, famed for many eminent graduates, including Ralph Waldo Emerson, was founded in 1634. In 1636, the principal inhabitants of Boston contributed from four shillings up to ten pounds each toward the maintenance of a free schoolmaster. In 1636, the General Court also appropriated four hundred pounds toward the establishment of a college for Massachusetts Bay. It was named for the Rev. John Harvard when the young Puritan minister who had a Master of Arts degree from Emmanuel College, Cambridge, died at thirty-one and left half his estate, nearly eight hundred pounds, and all of his library of four hundred books to the new college. Winthrop, Dudley, four other magistrates, and six ministers were named to Harvard's first Board of Overseers. The name of Newtown, where they bought one and one-eighth acres of land for Harvard's Yard, was changed to Cambridge in honor of Cambridge in England, where many of the Puritan leaders had been educated.

The entrance requirements to Harvard were specific. "When any scholar is able to understand Tully or such like Latin authors extempore, and make and speak true Latin . . . and decline perfectly the paradigms of nouns and verbs in the Greek tongue, let him then, and not before, be capable of admission to the college."

Harvard instituted a course of four years leading to the Bachelor of Arts degree; required another three years for its Master of Arts. Students had to read the Bible twice a day. They had to keep silent before their elders. They were fined for cursing, picking locks, or firing guns and pistols in the Yard. They were strictly forbidden to associate with ungodly persons.

On November 11, 1647, the General Court passed its "Old Deluder" act. Its intent was to thwart Satan, "that Old Deluder," to

"A Westerly View of the Colleges in Cambridge New England" includes from left to right Holden Chapel, Hollis College, Harvard Hall, Stoughton and Massachusetts colleges. The Massachusetts General Court appropriated the funds to establish Harvard in 1636, thereby initiating the private college idea in America

make it possible for men to read the Scriptures, and to ensure "that learning may not be buried in the grave of our fathers." The act ordered:

> . . . every township in this jurisdiction, after the Lord hath increased them to the number of fifty householders, shall then forthwith appoint one with their town to teach all such children as shall resort to him to read and write, whose wages shall be paid either by the parents or masters of such children, or by the inhabitants in general. . . .
>
> And it is further Ordered, that when any town shall increase to the number of one hundred families or householders, they shall set up a Grammar School, the master thereof being able to instruct youth as far as they may be fitted for the university.

Liberty and Law

For many years John Winthrop took no salary. When the colony could not supply funds, he spent his own money for public purposes. He neglected his own fortunes in his dedication to the affairs of Massachusetts. This very liberality made him enemies.

Then deputy-governor, Thomas Dudley found fault with Winthrop's administration. John Cotton and a committee of the clergy declared that Winthrop had been too lenient in his decisions as a magistrate and too mild in ordering punishments. After a dispute concerning the militia, the Hingham minister and his allies demanded a hearing before the General Court. They accused Winthrop of having exceeded his authority.

What has been called the attempted impeachment of John Winthrop ensued. Governor when the incident occurred, now deputy-governor, Winthrop voluntarily removed himself from the bench and took his place before the bar. After seven weeks of debate the General Court completely exonerated Winthrop and fined his accusers. Asked to retake his rightful place on the bench, John Winthrop asked "leave for a little speech." The character of the man shows through what he said with a lawyer's clarity and a statesman's

71

eloquence before the Court meeting May 24, 1645, in the First Church of Boston. Though obscured in the United States today, the principle which he enunciated is still valid.

There is a two-fold liberty,—natural (I mean as our nature is now corrupt), and civil or federal. The first is common to man with beasts and other creatures. By this, man as he stands in relation to man simply, hath liberty to do what he lists; it is a liberty to evil as well as to good. This liberty is incompatible and inconsistent with authority and cannot endure the least restraint of the most just authority. The exercising and maintaining of this liberty makes man grow more evil, and in time to be worse than brute beasts. . . . This is the great enemy of truth and peace, that wild beast, which all the ordinances of God are bent against, to restrain and subdue it.

The other kind of liberty I call civil or federal,—it may also be termed moral. . . . This liberty is the proper end and object of authority, and cannot subsist without it; and it is a liberty to that only which is good, just, and honest. . . . This liberty is maintained and exercised in a way of subjection to authority; it is the same kind of liberty wherewith Christ hath made us free.

CHAPTER FOUR

How the Massachusetts Colonists Lived

The conventional picture of the grim-faced Puritan in sober garb is a cartoonist's gibe. The English in colonial Massachusetts did not suffer unduly from repression, and they wore the brightly colored clothes worn in England at the time. They lived closely together in crowded houses. They spoke coarsely in the manner of the seventeenth century. They took few baths.

The people spilling off ships into already crowded Boston were idealists. Some were rebellious nonconformists. Many came not out of religious scruples at all but because they pulsed with energy that had made them brave the Atlantic in small ships. They came partly for the sheer excitement of it, largely in the hopes of bettering their fortunes.

They were strong, lusty, and determined or headstrong. The weak-willed and the spindly did not emigrate. Those who came were generally men and women of strong appetites and high animal spirits. If they did not have them, they did not come; or if they did come, they did not survive.

Massachusetts was thriving. Huts and one-room cottages were giving way to substantial homes of two stories with clapboarded sides and shingled roofs. Profitable cargoes of herring, cod, furs, and lumber were being shipped back to England. Tools, provisions, furniture, all kinds of necessities and even some luxuries were being imported. Merchants were beginning to grow rich. Hammering and sawing were continual in Boston, Salem, and other port towns as they developed.

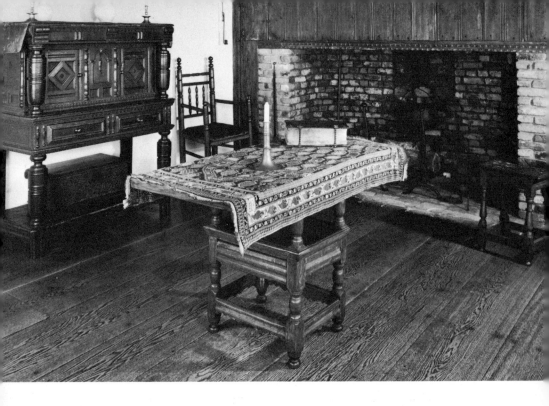

Parlor of the Thomas Hart House, built in Ipswich about 1640, can be seen now in New York's Metropolitan Museum Of Art. By that time, the settlers were able to import finer furniture and some luxuries for their homes

More and more immigrants came. Some remained in Boston. Others went to outlying towns or founded settlements of their own, building first a meeting house for church and town meetings. Lands were allotted them. Plowing, harrowing, cultivating, and reaping began. Men went hunting and fishing. Men were free to work and prosper as they could, free to govern themselves in the town meetings.

Excepting the clergy and magistrates, every man from sixteen to sixty had to serve in the militia. This was a necessity and a shared responsibility where Indians, not all of them friendly, still abounded. All, perforce, attended church on Sunday morning and again Sunday afternoon, but this was no chore for most. It was diversion. It was their social and intellectual life. They were intensely concerned with God, heaven, and hell as well as with Massachusetts Bay.

Though the clergy and the magistrates may have wished for it, propriety was no more rife in colonial Massachusetts than it is in most places at any time. There were those who professionally or personally admired it, but many were content to admire it from a safe distance. As always in a seaport, Boston had its rougher element. Other towns had their problems. In one, four excited servants hunted down and killed a raccoon while the congregation was at church. They were caught and punished. A man had to be fined for boating a cargo of hay from Gloucester into Marblehead on the Sabbath.

Throughout society there was a callousness to cruelty. Men did not invite or happily endure pain, but they were not averse to inflicting it or seeing it inflicted. Few were squeamish.

The Classes, Professions, and Trades

As nearly as they could the Massachusetts colonists duplicated the kind of life they had known in England. A man wanted his own home, his own wife, and plenty of children to help with the work. He expected to be ruled by gentlemen, but he wanted a say in which gentlemen should govern. He wanted his own land, and he was willing to fight for it. Disputes about property lines were constant. Quarrels were frequent. Somebody was usually suing somebody for infringement of his rights, for slander, or just to keep in practice.

About 80 percent of the people were farmers. Only about 2 percent were ruling gentlefolk. The gentry and the clergy were the aristocrats. Just below them came the merchants who, as they accumulated wealth in trade, had to be admitted to the ranks of power. The artisans and freehold farmers ranked next in the social scale. They voted in town affairs and held town offices. Below these came the journeymen of many crafts and the unskilled workers. The indentured servants, many of them working off their passage, were a fourth class; and below all were the few Indian or Negro slaves.

The colonial era was an age of specialization in the trades. These are woodcuts of a tin plate worker and button maker from the *Book of Trades,* published in the colonies in 1807 but imported from England much earlier

Many of the magistrates had had legal training and most of them knew theology. They were university educated. They knew the classics, and some read and spoke foreign languages. There were few lawyers in early Massachusetts, but the colony had physicians from the first. There were, of course, Congregational ministers in plenty. Some were pastors, others were "teachers." Most of the large churches had one of each.

In Boston by 1647 there were furriers, weavers, feltmakers, brick and tile makers, three kinds of leatherworkers, carpenters, joiners, and metal workers in seven different trades. Massachusetts had chandlers, sawyers, fullers, millers, tanners, bakers, and in every settlement the much-needed blacksmith. A shoemaker, Thomas Beard, brought his tools and materials with him on a voyage the *Mayflower* made in 1629. John Saunders was a bookbinder in Boston as early as 1637. A potter, Philip Drinker, was at work in 1635. Stephen Daye, who set up the first press in the colonies in the cellar of the president's house at Harvard, was also a locksmith.

As in England, farmers in the various towns lived in villages, usually around a town common where sheep and cows grazed, and had their tillage land outside the town, fields where they went each day to work. Massachusetts Bay granted land to groups of settlers, usually congregations, for village sites. The towns in turn gave householders home lots varying in size by rank and size of family, then outlying farm acreage. A man might have a few acres around his village home, then ten, twenty, or thirty acres afield.

Usually the first building erected in a village was the meeting house on the common. Near it the whipping post and stocks went up. All three could be seen from the farmers' homes. The farmers's tools were iron-tipped wooden broad hoes, spades, mattocks, and forks. Iron, which had to be imported at first, was scarce. The village usually had its shoemaker and its currier, and had to have its blacksmith. If a man wanted a nail, a hinge, a spike, or a tool, he had to have the blacksmith make it for him.

Soon there was more iron for the blacksmith to work. Bog iron was found in the Saugus ponds. John Winthrop, Jr., an energetic

The Blacksmith Shop in Pioneer Village, the reproduction of early Salem which provides a realistic picture of colonial life

figure in the colony, went to England, raised money, obtained skilled workers (men captured by Cromwell in the civil wars) and brought them to Massachusetts. He set up a furnace about 1642. By 1648 this mill was turning out eight tons of iron a week. Another mill was built in 1644 at Braintree.

Plymouth invited men from the Braintree operation to set up another mill and iron works in Taunton, where it opened in 1656. It made Taunton the most prosperous town in the Plymouth colony. Taxes and the schoolteacher's salary were paid in iron bars.

The Home

The house of one room built around its huge fireplace gave way to one-floor homes of several rooms, then to two-storied houses, rooms on the second floor matching those below. Most were clapboarded and shingled, with gabled roofs. Two-storied homes usually had the upper story projecting a foot or two over the lower. Some houses were "salt boxes," the roof sloping lower on one side than the other. Boston's wealthy built large, substantial houses, some of brick.

Inside the ordinary homes, floors were of wide boards, random width, scoured and sometimes with sand sprinkled on them. Furniture ran from the work of skilled artisans in Boston's fine homes to crude benches and tables in village houses. As no houses had closets, there were many chests, large and small, to hold clothing and household wares. Often there was a chest of drawers in the kitchen. Though the wealthy might have silver, most people ate from pewter dishes and ate with a spoon and their fingers. John Winthrop had a fork, a rare item in the colonies, which he kept in a case. There was some china imported from Holland or from the East India Company. Usually it was for display, and the farmer's wife showed her few pieces proudly on the kitchen dresser.

There were curtains in the parlors and bedrooms of the more prosperous families and chairs with leather or straw seats. Eight to ten feet wide and of heavy stone, the fireplace bore the spits and pothooks, and was hung with iron ladles and skillets. There was an oven in every chimney for baking beans and cornbread.

Food and Drink

The colonists ate well, families raising most of their vegetables themselves. They had peas, beans, cabbage, corn—always corn—but no potatoes as yet. They had bacon, beef, and fish of all kinds—cod, herring, mackerel, sturgeon, and in the coastal towns lobster and shellfish. Fruit was plentiful. The staple was always corn, called the Indian's best gift to the white man. The Massachusetts colonists ate it fresh from the cob, ground it into meal or made it into hominy. The first windmill for grinding corn was built near Boston. The first water mill was built in Dorchester in 1632. Hasty pudding, generally consumed, was cornmeal mush and milk.

Game was plentiful. Rural families found it in the woods and fields that pressed down on every settlement. People in the larger towns did not have to go far beyond the outskirts to hunt, and they could buy game cheaply at the fairs and markets. Venison was the beef of the time. For some years the colonists could not afford to slaughter cattle. All of the original stock had to be brought from England, and herds were not yet large enough to kill off any for eating. Deer, rabbit, wild turkey, geese, duck, and pigeons were easy to obtain. The Massachusetts colonists were hearty English, and they ate like hearty English men and women.

Every house had its own herb as well as vegetable garden. Herbs were raised for their medicinal as well as their food value and for scenting linen. Each home came to have its cow, or two or three or four. Farmers had their needed oxen for plowing, cultivating, removing stumps. Some soon had sheep, and almost always there were pigs.

After the first trying years, life was comparatively easy. As ships made port continually from Bristol and London, there was comfort and often luxury in the home.

There were no prohibitionists and few temperance men. The English colonists of Massachusetts were not water drinkers. Passengers on the *Mayflower,* the *Arbella,* and all the ships that followed had their beer, which they considered as much a necessity as bread. Every family had as much wine and aqua vitae (brandy or whisky) as it could obtain. Many ministers, deacons, and magistrates had limbecs, small stills for distilling cordials, in their homes. Drunkenness, not drinking, was a punishable offense and regularly attacked from the pulpit, but ministers drank and some got publicly drunk.

In the country towns, cider was served with every meal, and jugs of it were carried into the fields by farmers and farm hands to refresh themselves as they hoed or harvested. Even the elect did not despise cider. When he was president of Harvard, the Rev. Edward Holyoke used to lay in thirty barrels of cider every year for his family and many guests. In the late winter when the cider had fermented thoroughly, he poured a bottle of liquor into each barrel and had the resultant brew bottled. It must have been very potent.

Home Life

Men who farmed worked from dawn to dark at their chores and in the fields. Most families had servants, but the farm work was done by the farmer and his sons. They arose very early. Scripture reading came before breakfast, which was often porridge in wooden bowls. During the morning the women of the household cooked over log fires in the fireplace. Dinner, the big meal of the day, was at noon when the men came in from the fields. Pewter dishes were heaped with roast meats or succotash. Succotash was not just the mixture of beans and corn, which goes by the name today, but a substantial dish, really a stew, containing meat, peas, corn, and other vegetables.

At night there would be cold meat, bread, and beer or cider, with perhaps a hasty pudding for the children. Families were generally in bed by eight o'clock at night. This was the general regimen, broken

This is an artist's
conception of a Puritan
Christmas, a day suited more
for guarding against Indian
attacks than for celebrating

by town meetings, church on Sunday morning and afternoon, and midweek lecture, all of which must have seemed pleasant diversions. There were few other forms of entertainment. Massachusetts believed in work, not play. No wonder training days, when the militia turned out to drill on the common, usually turned into festive celebrations.

Every man had his gun, usually a flintlock now, and often a fowling piece as well. He had to provide his own arms and a supply of ammunition when he appeared on militia service. A man usually molded his own lead bullets, and his guns served not only for protection against possible Indian attacks, but also for supplying provender for his family.

Dress

Massachusetts colonists dressed like their counterparts in England, and it was a time when both men and women dressed colorfully. Laboring men wore leather and canvas or other coarse fabrics. The upper and middle classes had suits of doublets, waistcoats, and breeches. Restriction on display did not apply to those who could prove they had substantial incomes or property, and many who could afford it did their best to keep up with the latest London fashions. Some men wore coats trimmed with silver lace. Most wore bright waistcoats, cloaks of various colors, and often silver buttons on their coats.

Few in even early Boston and Plymouth wore black. Even Elder Brewster had a violet cloak, a blue cloth suit, a green waistcoat, and a lace cap. In the 1630s there were men who sported blue silk garters, worn outside over their hose just below the knee, with points dangling from them. Men wore long-sleeved linen shirts of white or various colors.

Women dressed in bright colors. They wore full, ankle-length skirts, tight bodices, caps, and often silk hoods. They had gowns and cloaks, shawls and scarves. They wore gold and silver rings and tortoise-shell combs in their hair. The clergy might rail, but laws have never long stifled normal human vanity and pleasure in self-adornment.

All kinds of cloth, some of it very rich, was imported from England. Colonists who could afford them had calico, cambric, challis, flannel, lawn, linen, serge, plush, silk, satin, and other clothing fabrics. The colonists themselves raised flax to spin and weave into linen, and they raised sheep for wool. Importing indigo from the Barbados and using sources at hand for other colors—as browns from hickory and oak bark, purple from iris, and orange from sassafras—they dyed their own fabrics. The first fulling mill to get close texture into homespun fabrics and to remove the grease, was started in Rowley in 1638 by twenty families from Yorkshire. Its success led to the establishment of other fulling mills and cloth manufactories in Dorchester, Roxbury, Watertown, Andover, Ipswich, and Salem.

Trade

People farmed, but the economy of colonial Massachusetts depended not on farming products but on fish, furs, and lumber.

Massachusetts exported quantities of these and imported cloth, tools, glass, metals, books, paper, and London necessities and luxuries. Legally the colony could trade only with England. In practice, Massachusetts did sea business wherever it could.

Fishing became the great industry in the Bay, Dorchester being the first town to begin large-scale fishing. By 1634, one merchant alone in Marblehead had eight fishing boats continually at work. Massachusetts Bay exported 300,000 dried fish in 1641. The one town of Marblehead sold 4,000 pounds worth in 1647. By 1666, Massachusetts had 1,300 fishing boats at work, and Salem, Ipswich, and Charlestown were centers for cod and mackerel fishing. Thousands of men were employed in the industry. The colony sent fish to Malaga, the Canary Islands, the Portugese Islands, and to Barbados. Catholic countries in Europe with their many fast days provided a large market for fish.

Allied to fishing was shipbuilding. As early as 1624, a professional ship's carpenter was sent from England to Plymouth where he began to build light, strong shallops which the Plymouth men used in coastal trading. Six shipwrights were sent to Salem in 1629 by the Massachusetts Bay Company even before it came to New England. About a year after landing, Governor John Winthrop launched the *Blessing of the Bay*, a sloop of 60 tons and the first sizable ship built in Massachusetts. It was the first Massachusetts ship to engage in trade with the Dutch at New Amsterdam. In 1645, according to Winthrop, Massachusetts sent its first ships to the fishing fleet at the Grand Banks. In 1636, the *Desire*, 120 tons, was built in Marblehead. Shipbuilding was soon under way in Boston, Dorchester, and Gloucester. Salem gloried in building the *Trial*, an enormous ship for the time, of 300 tons.

Massachusetts traders shipped cargoes of fish, fur, horses, and wood from New England. In the West Indies they took on molasses, indigo, and cotton. They sold these in the Chesapeake Bay region or New Amsterdam, took on tobacco and furs for England, and brought manufactured goods back to Massachusetts. Traders got rich on their ventures. Thousands of Massachusetts sailors and fishermen thrived as a result. Salem became a great seafaring port. Its sea captains were also merchants on an international scale. By 1700, there were 1,000 ships registered as having been built in New England.

Slavery

Very late in the seventeenth century and throughout the eighteenth, Massachusetts had still another profitable cargo. The first African slaves were brought to America by a Dutch privateer and sold with difficulty in Jamestown. As the demand for unskilled labor in the West Indies and in the agrarian southern colonies rose, the slave trade increased. Until the 1690s, it was a monopoly of the Royal African Company in England. Then everybody was in on it.

Negroes were enslaved in Africa by Africans who captured them in war or kidnapped them, then sold them on the Slave Coast of Africa to the traders of many nations. Massachusetts had few slaves —not for moral reasons but because it could not use them as could the cotton, rice, and tobacco plantations in the South.

Ships were loaded with rum and trade goods in New England and sailed to Africa where the cargo was exchanged for slaves. Sailing the notorious "Middle Passage," traders sold these in the West Indies for sugar and molasses which was made into rum in New England. There were about 50,000 Negro slaves in the American colonies by 1700.

Massachusetts colonists were not as color conscious as some of their descendants became or as the struggle for civil rights has made all Americans in the 1960s. Both black and white men were present on most occasions, a situation assumed as normal, thus often not recorded. Crispus Attucks gained his place in history. A Negro patriot in the colonial forces is thought to have fired the shot which killed Major John Pitcairn, commander of the Royal Marines in the Battle of Bunker Hill. The best-known marker in the burying ground in

Concord is that of John Jack, a Negro. He lies buried with the patriot leaders of the Concord fight.

Phillis Wheatley, a Negress of Boston and a slave, became a poetess whose work earned the praise of Benjamin Franklin and George Washington. Washington welcomed her to his Cambridge headquarters to thank her for a poem she had written about him. Her first book of poems was published in London in 1773. Lucy Terry of Deerfield, a Negress, wrote a rhymed account of the Indian attack on her village in 1746.

Phillis Wheatley was bought as a child by a Boston merchant, John Wheatley. Her Quaker mistress taught her to read and write, and her poetry received recognition in the colonies and in England

CHAPTER FIVE

Western Massachusetts

Two forces led to the early settlement of western Massachusetts, the region of the fertile Connecticut Valley and the densely wooded Berkshire Hills about one hundred miles overland—a long distance and a difficult journey in the seventeenth century—from the eastern shore. One was the bitter insistence of the Bay clergy on strict conformity to their views and their intolerance of any shadow of religious liberalism. The other force was the lure of quick profits to be made in the fur trade and the promise of rich farming land. Thus two widely separated parts of Massachusetts developed each in its own way while the intervening country long remained comparatively unsettled.

It seems strange now, but there was also the pressure of population. As Puritans continued to stream into Massachusetts until 1640, Boston and its neighboring towns grew crowded. Cotton Mather described conditions graphically in his *Magnalia Christi Americana:*

> It was not long before the Massachusetts colony was become like an hive overstocked with bees, and many of the new inhabitants entertained thoughts of swarming into plantations extended further into the country. . . . The fame of the Connecticut River, a long, fresh river, had made a little Nile of it, in the expectation of the good people of Massachusetts Bay. . . .

The "Quonektacut"—Indian name meaning "the long river"—rises in New Hampshire, forms a greater part of the boundary between New Hampshire and Vermont, and flows south through Massachusetts and Connecticut for 345 miles to empty into Long

Island Sound at Saybrook (named by the younger John Winthrop for Lord Say and Lord Brook who held a grant to land on the shore of the Sound). The river was known early to the English who sailed south around Cape Cod. Reports came back of bass, sturgeon, salmon, and shad in the river, of lush Indian corn grown in the Valley, of hemp growing in the region, and of beaver in plentiful supply available from the Indians.

In October 1633, a party of Plymouth men led by William Holmes sailed up the river to plant a trading post. The Dutch of New Amsterdam, who had learned of the plan, reached what is now Hartford, Connecticut, the day before and tried to stop them. Ignoring their menacing guns—which were not fired—the Plymouth men sailed on up to Windsor, just below what is now the boundary between Massachusetts and Connecticut. At Windsor, the Plymouth venturers built the first English homes in the Valley.

The next year the liberal and democratic Thomas Hooker sought leave of the General Court to move with part of his Newtown (Cambridge) congregation to the Connecticut Valley. In 1635, this permission was granted with the provision that the people remain under the jurisdiction of Massachusetts Bay. Another group under another leader had already made a preliminary survey of a site farther up the river, and two men had been sent ahead to build a house for the new plantation.

The Founding of Springfield

William Pynchon was one of the assistants who came over with John Winthrop on the *Arbella*. Great-grandson of Sir Richard Empson and uncle of the Countess of Portland, he had been a man of wealth and standing in England, where he was squire of Springfield, near Chelmsford, in Essex. He came first to Dorchester, where he remarried after the death of his first wife. He then founded Roxbury (first called Agawam) and became a leader in the fur trade. Treasurer of Massachusetts in 1633 and 1634, he was appointed one of the commissioners to govern the new settlements in the west.

William Pynchon's portrait and
signature, as well as a print of
"Old Fort Pynchon," the
original "house for the towne"
of Springfield. Fortified against
the Indians, it was the place
for worship and transaction of
town business

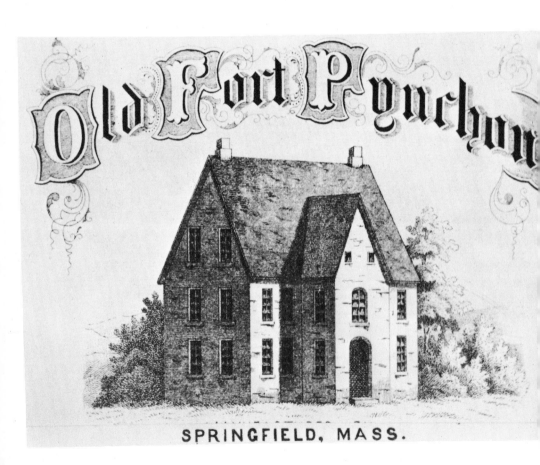

SPRINGFIELD, MASS.

A group of people in Roxbury decided to move to a spot on the Connecticut which Pynchon had selected and which Pynchon and two others are thought to have first visited in 1634. Two Roxbury men, John Cable and John Woodcock, were sent ahead to build a house on ground which had been cultivated by the Indians on the west side of the river, and the Pynchon party started out in 1636.

They sent their goods around the Cape and up the Connecticut in John Winthrop's *Blessing of the Bay,* but they marched overland. In May, they reached the top of the hill at Agawam overlooking the river and renamed the place Springfield after Pynchon's English estate. Eight men set up a government to which the others subscribed, and the first allotments of land were made.

The Indians of the Valley took their names from the places where they had their villages. The Agawams or river Indians were at Springfield (Agawam), the Woronokes at what became Westfield, the Nonotucks at Northampton, the Pocumtucks at Deerfield, and the Squakheags at Northfield. The Roxbury people purchased their land at Springfield from the Agawams, paying eighteen fathoms of wampum, eighteen coats, eighteen hoes, and eighteen knives. It was further agreed that the Indians could use the land freely, take game and fish from the river, and gather acorns and ground nuts on the land which had been theirs.

As in the coastal settlements, the Springfield settlers built their meeting house facing a town common and their houses around the common. They had their gardens on their home lots and their fields, meadows, and wood lots beyond. Pynchon was made magistrate and, in effect, the ruler of the community he had founded and in which he was the largest property holder. He built his warehouse on the river a few miles below Springfield at what is still called Warehouse Point. The furs, principally beaver, which he and his agents got from the Indians were packed in hogsheads and shipped down the river to the warehouse, thence to England.

Province of the Maſſachuſetts-Bay,

WILLIAM SHIRLEY, Eſq;
Captain-General and GOVERNOUR in Chief, in and
over His MAJESTY's Province of the *Maſſachuſetts-
Bay* in *New-England*, &c.

To *Phinehas Chapin Gentleman* ——— Greeting.

BY Virtue of the Power and Authority, in and by His Majeſty's Royal Commiſſion to
Me granted to be Captain General, &c. over this His Majeſty's Province of the *Maſſachuſetts-Bay*, aforeſaid; I (by theſe Preſents) repoſing eſpecial Truſt and Confidence
in your Loyalty, Courage and good Conduct, conſtitute and appoint You the ſaid
Phinehas Chapin ——— to be *Enſign of the Foot Company in the Town of Springfield*
——— under the command of
Captain Ebenezer Hitchcock ——— in the *South* Regiment of Militia within
the County of *Hampshire* ——— whereof *....... ....* Eſq; Colonel. ———

You are therefore carefully and diligently to diſcharge the Duty of an *Enſign*
in leading, ordering and exerciſing ſaid *Company* ——— in Arms, both inferiour Officers and
Soldiers, and to keep them in good Order and Diſcipline; hereby commanding them to obey you
as their *Enſign* ——— and your ſelf to obſerve and follow ſuch Orders and Inſtructions, as
you ſhall from time to time receive from Me, or the Commander in Chief for the Time being, or
other your ſuperior Officers for His Majeſty's Service, according to military Rules and Diſcipline,
purſuant to the Truſt repoſed in You.

Given under My Hand & Seal at Arms at Boſton, the *Twenty Eighth* ———
Day of *August* ———, in the *Twenty Eighth* ——— Year of the Reign of His
Majeſty King GEORGE the Second, Annoq; Domini, 1754.

By His EXCELLENCY's
Command, *J. Willard Secry*   *W Shirley*

This commission dates from the eighteenth century, yet long before that men
banded together formally to protect the settlements of western Massachusetts

A hundred miles from rigid Boston, Springfield was largely independent. With his sons-in-law, Elizer Holyoke and Henry Smith,
and the minister, George Moxon, Pynchon governed a fairly democratic community. He sat in judgment on cases for breach of contract, thieving, slanders, and the varied disputes arising in a frontier
settlement. One case of witchcraft came before him in 1645.

According to Pynchon's records, "the widow Marshfield complained against Mary H., wife of Hugh Parsons of Springfield, for
reporting her to be suspected for a witch, and she produced Jo Mat-
thews and his wife for her witnesses." Tried first for slander, Goody
Parsons was found to be the witch herself. She had tried to divert
attention from her evil doing by accusing another. She was then

publicly charged with bewitching the minister's children. Later the poor, half-demented woman killed her infant child. She was sent on to Boston to be tried for both murder and witchcraft and found guilty by a jury. The magistrates did not concur, and the General Court dismissed the case. The condemned woman is thought to have died in prison.

Founding of Northampton

Largely in a move to expand their fur trade, William Pynchon, Samuel Pynchon, and Elizer Holyoke petitioned the General Court for permission to found a settlement at Nonotuck about twenty miles further up the Connecticut. Under an agreement of 1654 with Wawhilloa, Basicohee, Nenessahalant, and four other Nonotuck Indians, they purchased what became Northampton for one hundred fathoms of wampum, two coats, some small gifts, and the promise to plow sixteen acres of land on the east side of the river for the Indians the following spring. The usual "house for the town" was built and settlement begun by families from Springfield and from Hartford, Weathersfield, and Windsor in Connecticut.

Northampton's oldest home, the Cornet Joseph Parsons House dates from 1658, four years after the city's land was purchased from the Indians

Every original settler received four acres of meadow, every family head six acres. The twenty men who had paid for the land got one-fourth of about eight hundred acres of intervale owned by the town. Later settlers were given grants of house and meadow lots on condition they would cultivate them for a year.

Laws adopted in Springfield regulated most transactions. Laborers' wages were set at sixteen shillings a day in winter, twenty in summer. Lowest paid of all skilled workers, tailors got only twelve pence a day. Springfield and the towns founded from it—Hadley, Hatfield, Whately, Deerfield, and Northfield after Northampton—each had selectmen (select townsmen), highway surveyors, fence viewers, and a swineringer. As hogs were allowed to roam free, their noses were ringed to prevent their grubbing. Springfield and Hadley (at first written "Hadleigh") both sent deputies to the Massachusetts General Court in Boston.

Every male over fifteen was a soldier and had to appear for muster once a month on training day. Until they were sixty they were liable for the forces of the New England Confederation, which was made up of Plymouth, Massachusetts Bay, Connecticut, and New Haven. Urged by John Winthrop, strongly seconded by Thomas Hooker, the Confederation, founded in 1643 "for mutual safety and welfare" was the first step toward a federal union. With about fifteen thousand people and the greatest resources, Massachusetts was the dominant member. The other colony members had only about two thousand people each.

A familiar figure led the combined military force. Josiah Holland quoted an unnamed record. "The first Major General was the much honored Thomas Dudley, Esquire, whose faithfulness and great zeal, and love to the truths of Christ, caused the people to choose him to this office, although he were far stricken in years."

Relations with the Indians

Indian relations in the Massachusetts segment of the Connecticut Valley were at first friendly. The English had preempted land burnt over, cleared, and cultivated by the Indians. They selected what had been the choice sites of the Indians for their domains. They used the well-worn Indian paths from one Indian village to another, and they depended on the Indians for the furs which were bringing Pynchon and his associates new fortunes. As they had done in the first years at Plymouth, the two civilizations lived side by side and made what seem to have been honest attempts to respect each other's rights.

In many places the Indians were allowed to live undisturbed on lands they had just sold to the English. There was one Indian village on the southern border of Springfield, another on the banks of the Connecticut there. The Indians had a strong fortress on Long Hill about a mile and a half south of Springfield.

The Nonotucks asked permission to build a fort at Northampton. Permission was granted on the following terms:

> . . . that the Indians do not work, game, or carry burdens within their town on the Sabbath; nor powwow here nor anywhere else; nor get liquor or cider, nor get drunk; nor admit Indians from without the town; nor break down the fences of the inhabitants; not let cattle or swine upon their fields, but go over a stile at one place . . . nor hunt or kill cattle, sheep or swine with their dogs.

Except for the Sabbath restriction the settlers tried to place on their non-Puritan neighbors, the terms seem fair enough.

Downriver things had not been so peaceable a few years earlier. In 1633 the Pequot Indians at the mouth of the Connecticut murdered a drunk and dissolute Captain Stone, who had probably given them provocation. A year later, the Pequots, who were at war with the Narragansetts, sent emissaries to Boston. To ensure peace with the English, they gave up all rights to Connecticut and agreed to give up the two Indians who had killed Stone. In 1636, Narragansetts murdered John Oldham, early explorer of the Connecticut, off Block Island in Long Island Sound and seized his ship. They also captured two small boys whom Roger Williams persuaded them to release.

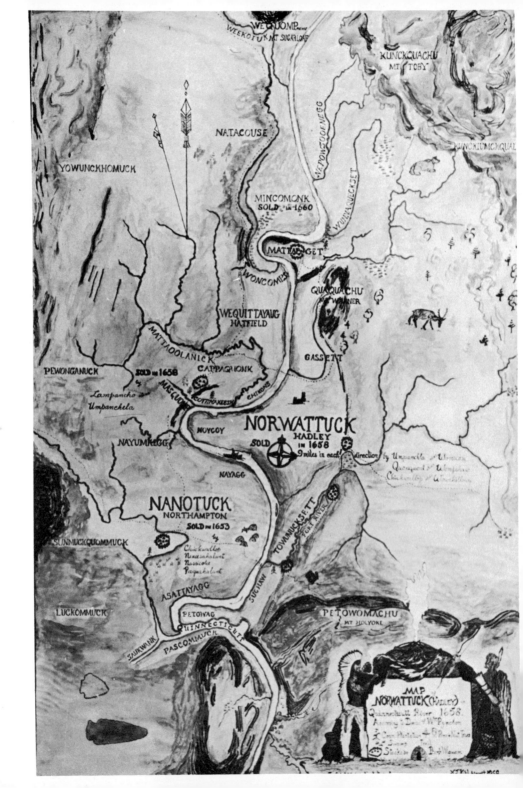

In reprisal, Massachusetts sent John Endecott with a hundred men and orders to put to death all the Indians on Block Island. Endecott could not find the Indians, who were hiding in the brush, so he burned down all their wigwams, destroyed their stores, smashed their canoes, killed all their dogs, and left victorious.

He then went to the mainland, demanded that the Pequots give up the murderers, spoiled their corn, killed about twenty of them, and demanded damages. According to Thomas Hutchinson, Lyon Gardiner, who commanded Saybrook Fort said bitterly, "You come hither to raise these wasps about my ears; then you will take wing and flee away."

Endecott had accomplished just what Gardiner feared. The enraged Pequots sought revenge in any way they could. They murdered and pillaged; they captured and tortured stray Englishmen. Connecticut appealed to Plymouth and Massachusetts for aid, and Massachusetts sent John Underhill with a small force and some Mohican allies. John Mason led ninety Connecticut men. Several hundred Narragansetts and Niantics joined them.

In May 1637, their Indian allies falling back through superstitious fear, seventy-seven colonials encircled the Pequot fort near what is now Stonington. There were four to five hundred Indian men, women, and children inside the enclosure of several acres. The Indians had only bows and arrows against the firearms of the whites. John Mason set fire to the fort. Many of the Pequots were burned alive. Those who attempted to escape by climbing to the top of the sapling palisade or rushing the narrow apertures at either end of the fortress, the English methodically shot down. Their Indian allies happily tomahawked any who somehow escaped fire or bullets.

It was a merciless slaughter. The English hunted down and captured any survivors and either killed or sold them into slavery in

Map of the "Quinnecticutt" River region, 1658, is based on the deeds of William Pynchon and shows the locations of corn plantations, swamps, stockades, nut trees and wigwams with appropriate symbols

Bermuda. Mason and Underhill were the heroes of the occasion, and their action was praised and applauded. Massachusetts and Connecticut had wiped out a threat to their existence. It delighted all those who cut off the heads and hands of Indians and set them up on poles in the towns to enrage the natives—then were surprised and indignant when the Indians returned the favor in the best way they knew by scalping any white men they could surprise.

Departure of Pynchon

Western Massachusetts was distinct from the Massachusetts seaboard, and long remained so. The Connecticut River was a wide and busy highway leading directly to the outside world. Furs could be shipped straight to England. The Valley towns depended for little on Boston. Just as they developed largely self-sufficient agricultural economies, they developed an independent spirit.

William Pynchon was not only magistrate in Springfield and a powerful figure throughout the Valley, but also an assistant of Massachusetts Bay until 1651. Then he made a mistake. He turned author. He wrote and had printed in London *The Meritorious Price of Our Redemption,* a theological pamphlet in which he attacked some orthodox Puritan views. Even from one of the original assistants, Massachusetts Bay could not permit such a liberty.

Pynchon's pamphlet was denounced by the Boston clergy. The General Court condemned it as heretical. Pynchon made some slight retractions but not enough to satisfy the clerical and lay authorities. His pamphlet was burned in public; twice he was ordered to appear before the General Court and confess to the rest of his theological errors. He was not reelected an assistant.

Pynchon, who had established western Massachusetts, even fighting off the attempts of Connecticut to annex Springfield, had had enough. A rich man grown richer, he deeded all his properties to his twenty-six year old son—a child of two when he sailed with his

This mill site deed of William Pynchon dates from 1651, and its original is preserved in the Northfield Museum

mother and father and John Winthrop from Southampton—and left. In 1652, with his wife and the minister John Moxon, he abandoned intolerant New England for more tolerant England.

CHAPTER SIX

King Philip's War

The Massachusetts colonists used and abused the Indians. They dispossessed them under various legal guises, cheated them in trades, and, though it was against their own laws, sold them guns and plied them with liquor. To protect themselves, they encouraged the Indians in their wars among themselves. They called the Indians ignorant savages, then tried to make them conform to their puritanical codes and customs and punished them if they did not. When hostilities broke out between whites and Indians, the colonists repaid savagery with calculated atrocities, doing it all for the glory of God and for their own safety and profit.

Yet there were those among the English who treated the Indians fairly and did their best to civilize them by white men's standards and to convert them to Christianity. Outstanding among these men was the Rev. John Eliot.

The "Apostle to the Indians"

Graduate of Jesus College, Cambridge, John Eliot, who came to Massachusetts Bay in 1631 and became teacher of the church in Roxbury, was a student of languages. With the help of a young Indian prisoner he began to learn the native language and began preaching to the Indians in their own tongue in 1646. That same year Massachusetts ordered that the churches should send two men each year to spread the gospel among the natives. In 1649 the Society for the

Propagation of the Gospel in New England was established in England and sent over several thousand pounds to further the work.

The Indians were not always easily convinced. Those on Nantucket and Martha's Vineyard told Thomas Mayhew that they were not stupid enough to barter thirty-seven gods for one, but the missionaries made headway, and many Indians professed at least nominal acceptance of Christian ideas and ideals. John Eliot aroused interest in his work through tracts which were circulated in Massachusetts and in England, and prepared an Indian grammar. In 1661 and 1663, he published the Old and New Testaments in the Massachusetts Indian language, a remarkable feat. The first Bible printed in North America was thus in Indian.

Because he believed the Indians fared best when living apart from the English, Eliot established a town of several Christianized Indian

The Reverend John Eliot and his guest, Father Druillettes, with three Christianized or "Praying" Indians in the background. Reverend Eliot prepared a grammar and bible for the Indians and also set up villages for them

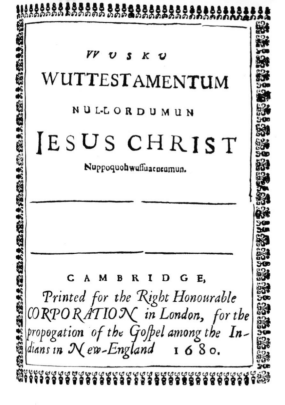

WUSKU
WUTTESTAMENTUM
NUL-LORDUMUN
JESUS CHRIST
Nuppoquohwuſſuaeneumun.

CAMBRIDGE,
Printed for the Right Honourable
CORPORATION in London, for the
propogation of the Goſpel among the Indians in New-England 1680.

Title page of one of the later editions of John Eliot's New Testament for the Indians, the first Bible printed in North America in 1661

families in Natick. Though under the jurisdiction of Massachusetts, it was practically a self-governing community. Later more villages of "Praying Indians" were founded adjacent to Massachusetts towns; near Concord, Grafton, in Plymouth colony, and on the islands of Nantucket and Martha's Vineyard. By 1674 there were fourteen such villages of Christianized Indians, an estimated four thousand people, who were, in general, loyal to the English.

The accomplishments of John Eliot and of Major Daniel Gookin, superintendent of the Praying Indians, were soon destroyed.

Plymouth's Indian Policy

Though it was settled ten years earlier, Plymouth never developed as did Massachusetts Bay. It lacked a harbor comparable to Boston's; the land was poor. It depended first on fur trade with the Indians, then on supplying richer and more populous Boston with corn and cattle. This necessitated geographical expansion. Needing more land to grow corn and raise cattle, men moved from the town of Plymouth to establish new settlements in the surrounding countryside.

Though Elder Brewster and William Bradford objected to this weakening of the original church and town, Miles Standish, John Alden, and Jonathan Brewster moved to Duxbury and founded a church there. Scituate was founded by Puritans who came from England and settled within the limits of Plymouth colony.

Plymouth town so declined that its leaders seriously considered moving the community to Eastham on Cape Cod. Bridgewater and Marshfield were founded. Families from Scituate, which prospered through having a fulling mill and a sawmill, moved to Barnstable on Cape Cod.

Plymouth people were somewhat more liberal than their neighbors to the north, suffering Roger Williams, Quakers, and even Baptists, but they were liberal only by comparison. Because they were weaker, they were more cautious and more severe in their dealings with the Indians. It was Plymouth which provoked—or at least, helped bring about—the bitter, bloody, and costly King Philip's war.

King Philip

William Brewster died in 1644; William Bradford in 1657. In 1661 Massasoit died, and the Wampanoags, who had kept their word and the peace for a half century, were led by Massasoit's son Wamsutta (or Alexander). Peremptorily summoned to appear before the General Court of Plymouth to answer to rumors that he planned hostilities, Wamsutta died of fever before he could get back to his people, and his brother, Philip, became chief sachem of the Wampanoags.

Philip has been pictured as a hero and as vain, extravagant, and cowardly. Early historians castigated the Indians as wholly responsible for the outbreak of violence. Others see the colonists as having made the conflict inevitable.

King Philip of Mount Hope, whose name has been given to the war that destroyed the Indian way of life in Massachusetts, and cost Massachusetts a considerable number of lives, towns, and pounds

Growing rapidly in numbers and in power, the colonists had encroached from the beginning on what the first inhabitants of Massachusetts had held theirs. As more towns sprang up—and there were about ninety in Massachusetts now—and these towns grew, the Indians were pushed back from the best lands along the coast and in the Connecticut Valley. Outnumbered and compressed willy-nilly in the wilderness between the two regions, they were forced to live by English law, which few of them understood. They saw their game being exterminated, their fields usurped by white men, their tribal way of life threatened.

The prospering Massachusetts colonists saw the Indians as an unavoidable evil, a nuisance to be got out of the way of progress. They saw them as a constant threat to the lives of people in outlying towns, even, should they decide to raid or ambush, to those in the older towns near Boston itself.

Overt trouble began at Taunton in 1671 when Philip was forced to sign a confession which read in part, "through my indiscretion and the naughtiness of my heart . . . I have violated and broken my covenant." Despite the treaty, the English continued to encroach on his lands, and the natural ire of the Indians grew. Writing more than ten years later, John Eliot and Daniel Gookin asked simply, "Was not a principal cause of the late war, about encroachments on Philip's land at Mount Hope?"

Later in 1671, Philip was arrested and taken to Plymouth. Though there was no evidence against him, he was made to pay forty pounds to defray the expenses of the expedition sent to arrest him. The Wampanoags were forced to surrender all their firearms. Philip had to sign a treaty acknowledging himself subject to Plymouth as well as to England. When he tried to get back the confiscated guns of his tribe, he found that the Plymouth authorities had simply distributed them among the settlers in its towns.

Angrily, Philip said, "My father gave them what they asked; they have had townships and whole Indian kingdoms for a few blankets, hoes, and flattering words; but they are not content;—the white man's throat is wide." Plotting revenge for indignities suffered and an end to the depredations of the colonists, Philip sought allies among the powerful Narragansetts and the Nipmucks of the Connecticut Valley. Though he tried, he could not arouse the Mohicans or the Praying Indians. His allies began to gather around him at Mount Hope (Bristol, Rhode Island).

A Praying Indian named Sausamon, who had studied for a time at Harvard, warned the Plymouth leaders of Philip's plot. Sausamon was promptly murdered by the Indians as a traitor and his body thrown into a lake. Plymouth executed the two Wampanoags who had killed him and a third who had been a witness.

A white man shot and wounded an Indian in Swansea, June 24,

1675. In retaliation, the Indians sacked Swansea and set it afire. By this time the troops of the New England Confederacy had taken the field in what would be an all-out war in Massachusetts. Philip intended to destroy the English. The English intended to exterminate the Wampanoags, Nipmucks, and Narragansetts as they had wiped out the Pequots forty years earlier.

At this time there were about sixty thousand colonists in New England and about thirty-six thousand Indians. The Indians had only about ten thousand warriors, the English about fifteen thousand fighting men. The colonists had the men and the firepower; the Indians had the strategical advantage of their guerrilla tactics of raid and ambush.

There was no quarter in this war. The Indians massacred, tortured, and beheaded. The English slaughtered, even murdering innocent Praying Indians, cut off heads, and generally equalled their foe in ferocity. The Indians struck Taunton, Middleborough, and Mendon. They laid seige to Brookfield where about one hundred men, women, and children had taken refuge. When Colonel Edward Hutchinson, eldest son of Anne Hutchinson, was sent to negotiate with the Nipmucks, they treacherously ambushed and killed him and eight other men with whom they had agreed to parley.

In the Connecticut Valley, Northfield had to be abandoned, and Deerfield was evacuated, but this did not prevent the famous Bloody Brook Massacre of September 12, 1675. For safety, the people had been taken to Hadley, the headquarters of the beleaguered English. On the morning of September 11, eighteen wagons and farmers returned to Deerfield to finish threshing their wheat. They were escorted by "the Flower of Essex," a train-band of ninety of the best-drilled soldiers in Massachusetts. After a night march, they were attacked from ambush the next morning as they forded a shallow stream. Most of them were killed.

Springfield, Northampton, and Hadley were attacked. At Hadley, a militia captain reported that, as ordered, he had had an old Indian woman torn to pieces by dogs. Medfield and Groton were attacked. Lancaster was burned. Sixteen houses in Plymouth itself were burned by the Indians.

Victory at Mount Hope

Fearful that the powerful Narragansetts would throw in their forces with Philip, one thousand colonists under command of Governor Josiah Winslow of Plymouth, marched to attack the Narragansett stronghold at Mount Hope, where about two thousand Indian men, women, and children were sheltered inside a palisaded enclosure. Although it was the Sabbath, Winslow decided to attack on December 16, 1676, and Massachusetts men rushed the blockhouse of the Indian fort under heavy fire. Six captains and many of their men were killed. More were wounded. Despite fierce resistance, the colonists took the garrison and set it afire. Perhaps one thousand Indians perished from gunfire or flames as the colonists filled that Sunday afternoon with precision slaughter.

It was a costly victory. Nearly one-quarter of the English were killed. It was also an incomplete victory. The Narragansett chieftain, Canonchet—whose father Miantonomo had sheltered Roger Williams after his banishment—escaped with a force of his warriors. They joined the Nipmucks in the Connecticut Valley.

The next spring Canonchet returned to get seed corn for his people. He was captured and condemned to death. In his *Narrative of the Trouble with the Indians in New England*, 1677, even the Indian-hating William Hubbard shows his admiration. When told of his sentence, Canonchet said, "he liked it very well that he should die before his heart was soft, or he had spoken anything unworthy of himself." As a concession, the colonists decided that he was not to be tortured. They turned Canonchet over to the zealous Mohicans, who tomahawked him.

Mary Rowlandson

Mary Rowlandson, wife of the minister of Lancaster, and three of her children were captured when Indians fired their home February 10, 1676. Two children were taken from her. She was allowed to carry the youngest who had been severely wounded. The small girl died, and Mrs. Rowlandson was made the slave of Weetamoo, chief of the Pocassets.

For three months of cold, hunger, and humiliation she was dragged about by the fleeing Indians. The Indians treated her well but had little themselves. At first she was revolted by what the Indians ate: snakes, bark, acorns. She found it, ". . . very hard to get down their filthy trash. But the third week, though I could think how formerly my stomach would turn against this or that and how I would starve and die before I could eat such things, yet they were sweet and savoury to my taste." She made a shirt and then a cap for King Philip's small boy. He gave her a shilling with which she bought a piece of horseflesh and then invited her to a dinner of a pancake of parched wheat beaten and fried in bear's grease. In her famous ac-

Knife (actual size 8″) and spearhead (5″) from the Rodimon Collection were discovered in the Connecticut Valley

count of her adventures Mrs. Rowlandson says, "I thought I never tasted pleasanter meat in my life." Philip offered her a pipe of tobacco but though, like most men and women, she had been a habitual pipe smoker, Mrs. Rowlandson forswore this indulgence during her captivity.

She was with the Indians when they attacked Northampton and other towns. This raiding went on everywhere, and the Massachusetts colonists retaliated in kind. In Marblehead a mob of women killed two innocent Praying Indians. At Turners Falls in the Connecticut Valley a captain for whom the town is named and his men killed three hundred Nipmucks whom they had surprised. A captain and seventy of his men were ambushed and fifty of them were slaughtered near Sudbury.

Following successful negotiations by John Hoar of Concord and two Christian Indians, Mrs. Rowlandson was freed on payment of twenty pounds to her captors. She rejoined her husband in Boston where the Old South Church provided them with a home.

Death of King Philip

Despite their concerted efforts and their devastating hit-and-run tactics, the Indians were gradually being crushed by weight of numbers, heavier firepower, and the murderous determination of the Puritans to destroy them. The war came to an end in Massachusetts when Captain Benjamin Church of Plymouth and a small force of friendly Indians hunted Philip down in neutral Rhode Island to which he had returned.

Betrayed by an Indian whose brother Philip had tomahawked for advising him to make peace, Philip was surprised near Mount Hope, August 12, 1676. One of Church's Indians shot him through the heart as he attempted to escape. His gun under him, Philip pitched forward into the mud and swamp water. He was dragged through the muck, then his body was quartered and hung in the trees. Later his head was cut off and sent to Plymouth, which displayed its prize on a pole erected on the village common. Philip's dead eyes watched the people of Plymouth walk to the meeting house for a special service of Thanksgiving.

Both Massachusetts Bay and Plymouth suffered heavily from King Philip's War. From twelve to sixteen towns were completely wiped out. Forty towns were severely damaged. More than six hundred men, military leaders of the two colonies, and one-tenth of their fighting forces were killed. Almost every family suffered casualities. Families which had lost their homes were living as refugees with other families. Some of the devastated towns were not rebuilt for years. The war cost Massachusetts Bay over forty-six thousand pounds and smaller Plymouth nearly twelve thousand. Property losses throughout New England were estimated at a half million pounds.

Fate of the Indians

The New England Confederation smashed the remaining Indian power and any chance of a new Indian conspiracy. The Narragansett, Wampanoag, and Nipmuck tribes were destroyed, and with them the Indian way of life in Massachusetts. More than two thousand Indians were killed, and the conquerors were harsh in their punishment of the survivors. They executed many sachems and warriors as war criminals. They dispersed Indian women and children throughout the colonies as serfs and servants. In Plymouth, where the captives were shipped for disposal, the General Court decreed that all male Indians be sold into slavery outside New England.

John Eliot wrote the commissioners of the Confederation, "To sell souls for money seemeth to me dangerous merchandise." The tough Indian fighter Benjamin Church warned that such action would make it more difficult to pacify the remaining Indians. Such protests were of no avail. Most complained only that the prices they got for the Indians were too low.

The Massachusetts colonists sold hundreds of Indians into slavery in the West Indies. When they could not find purchasers for their merchandise—many planters thought that Indians who had roamed the New England forests as hunters and had fought as warriors would not make good slaves—they simply abandoned them on strange shores. One boatload of Indians the Puritans took to the notorious slave marts of Morocco.

Among those enslaved were King Philip's wife and the small son for whom Mary Rowlandson had made the cap. Important churchmen, including the Rev. Increase Mather, teacher of Boston's Second Church and who was to become president of Harvard, did not approve. They advised that the boy be killed.

Found in Northampton, this Indian bi-pointed pottery jar has an ear of maize on each point

CHAPTER SEVEN

The Province of Massachusetts

From their settlement, both Plymouth and Massachusetts Bay had had much their own way. Massachusetts Bay in particular acted almost as a sovereign state. It made and enforced its own laws. It decided who could vote and who could not. It established its state religion. Both colonies maintained their own fighting forces. They fought their own wars without interference—or at this time help of any kind—from England.

At the restoration of the monarchy in England in 1660, Puritanism went out of office. Once it was convinced that the reign of Cromwell's commonwealth and the Long Parliament were over, Massachusetts tactfully sent protestations of its undying loyalty to Charles II. It then blithely continued to do as it pleased.

Too busy with its own affairs at home to pay much attention to the comparatively unimportant affairs of Massachusetts, England let things slide. About 1680, England decided to bring overly independent Massachusetts to heel. It issued sharp orders which were ignored, so it sent warships and British officials to Boston. England demanded money from Massachusetts to help fight the Dutch in New York. Massachusetts made show of obedience but little more. England lost patience. In 1684, the Court of Chancery invalidated the charter of the Massachusetts Bay Company and appointed Joseph Dudley provisional governor of Massachusetts, New Hampshire, and other parts of New England.

Son of the stern and self-righteous Thomas Dudley, this Dudley was an ambitious politician. A Harvard graduate, he had held many colonial offices, fought in the King Philip's War, and served as one of the colony's agents sent to London in an effort to save the charter. Massachusetts had always elected its own governors; now it was to be ruled by the appointee of a strange king. People looked upon Joseph Dudley as a traitor. Worse was to come.

Sir Edmund Andros

Supplanting Dudley and his temporary government, Sir Edmund Andros arrived in Boston in 1686 as royal governor of a domain that included Massachusetts Bay, Plymouth, Maine, New Hampshire, and King's Province, which was the Narragansett Bay country in Rhode Island. With him Andros brought red-coated British soldiers and surpliced priests of the Church of England. Installed in Province House with all the pomp and ceremony of a British official, he instituted Church of England services in the Old South Meeting House and began to collect taxes for the crown. The colonists, he declared, did not own the land on which they had built their towns and homes or the fields they farmed.

The protest was loud and shrill. Andros was a usurper and a tyrant! Merchants, artisans, tradesman, farmers, laborers, the churchly and the unrepentant all cried out against the new authority. Andros ignored their protests. Massachusetts dispatched the Rev. Increase Mather to England to try and regain the lost charter.

Neither protests in Boston nor the machinations of Mather in England but a revolution in England put an end to the regime of Sir Edmund Andros. When Charles II died in 1685, he was succeeded by James II. King James was driven from the throne and fled to France in 1688. William of Orange and his wife Mary, daughter of James II, were proclaimed king and queen of Great Britain on February 13, 1689.

Massachusetts, which had been on the verge of open rebellion, did not wait for official confirmation when the news reached Boston.

Militia raced in from outlying towns to join an armed mob in the streets. They seized the British frigate in the harbor. They imprisoned Andros in his own fort. For good measure they also incarcerated Joseph Dudley.

In a minor revolution eighty-six years before she fomented a larger one, Massachusetts dethroned England's government and reinstated her own exactly as it had been under the lost charter. It did not last long.

The Charter of 1691

A soldier, a Protestant, politically a liberal, King William III was more amenable to suggestion than James II had been. He wished the support of the New England colonies in England's wars against France and enforcement of the Navigation Acts which made her colonies a source of profit to England. Beyond this he was willing to listen to any reasonable proposals, and those which Increase Mather

Top portion of the original Massachusetts charter of 1628, which was invalidated by England in 1684, then replaced in 1691

made were very liberal for what had been an unmitigated theocracy. Mather was unable to get the original Massachusetts charter back, but he made substantial gains for the colony in the new charter which King William signed October 7, 1691.

Under this charter the king appointed a royal governor for the Province of Massachusetts, which now included Massachusetts Bay, Plymouth, Maine, and for a time Nova Scotia. Under the governor and his aides would be a Council or upper house of twenty-eight members and a lower house whose members would be elected annually by Massachusetts freeholders voting in town meetings. The possession of property rather than church membership was made the qualification for the franchise. The new charter also provided that "Forever hereafter there shall be a liberty of conscience allowed to the worship of God to all Christians."

Constitutions and charters are made to be interpreted and manipulated for their own advantage by those who can. A skilled politican as well as a Puritan divine, Increase Mather managed to get the man of his choice appointed the first royal governor under the 1691 charter.

Sir William Phips

A Maine ship's carpenter who plied his trade in Boston, William Phips became a ship's captain and a shipowner. He persuaded James II to outfit a ship to hunt sunken Spanish treasure off Hispaniola (Haiti). The gamble failed, but when Phips skippered a second expedition backed by the Duke of Albermarle he recovered three hundred thousand pounds in treasure. Phips was knighted for this achievement. He was made provost marshal general of Massachusetts and led successful expeditions of Massachusetts militia against the French in Canada. Failing in a second attempt, he went to England to seek support for a third try. There he became an ally of Increase Mather in obtaining the new charter.

Mather urged Phips' appointment as Massachusetts governor on

$N^o.$ (4980) 5^s

THIS Indented bill of Five shillings.
due from the Massachusets Colony to
the Possesor shall be in value equal to
money & shall be accordingly accepted,
by the Treasurer & receivers subordinate
to him in all publick payments and for
any Stock at any time in the Treasury
Boston in New-England, December
the 10th 1690; By Order of ye General
Court.

John Phillips
Adam Winthrop   } Comtee
Ann Townsend

SIGILVM: GVB: & SOC:
DE: MATTACHVSETS:
BAY: IN: NOV: ANGL:

Paper money was first issued in America in 1690. Sir William Phips returned with his troops after an unsuccessful expedition against Canada. The Governor was unprepared to pay the soldiers who were on the point of mutiny, so paper notes were issued by the General Court

William III, and the king made the appointment. From Mather's viewpoint, Phips was ideal. He was a soldier and had been a magistrate; he was in favor in England. Best of all, he was a member of Mather's son's congregation in the Second Church.

Phips should have been completely controllable by the Mather faction. Though some of his actions pleased the older order, Phips proved to be much his own man. He favored taxing everyone to support the established Congregational church, but he connived at thwarting many of the English laws he was sworn to uphold. A shipowner and trader, he was for free trade, not just for trade with England. Like most Massachusetts sea captains, he had nothing against a little profitable smuggling. When the Boston collector of customs attempted to seize a vessel suspected of illegal trading, Phips seized him instead and dragged him bodily around the wharf. He publicly caned a captain of the royal navy for refusing to obey him.

In the end, Phips was recalled to England to face charges, but before that he put an abrupt end to the Salem Witchcraft Trials of 1692.

Witchcraft

In the late seventeenth century witchcraft was not considered a delusion, a superstition, or a joke. In the minds of theologians, scientists, and the law in Europe as well as in the colonies it was a fearful Satanic fact. Belief in witchcraft was almost universal. Everyone knew that witches consorted with the devil. They were evil spirits who cast malignant spells over the helpless and tormented the innocent.

Often torture was used to extract confessions which led to gruesome executions. Joan of Arc was executed as a witch in 1431. Witches were executed in England and in Scotland. They were put to death under Elizabeth I, James I, and Cromwell. In 1664, under Charles II, when Sir Matthew Hale, Baron of the Exchequer, sentenced two women accused of witchcraft to death, the learned physician Sir Thomas Browne concurred in the sentence.

Springfield had its witchcraft case in 1645. In Boston, ten years later, a Mrs. Ann Hibbins was tried as a witch. Her husband, who had died the year before, had been an assistant and a Massachusetts agent in England. After his death and the loss of much of his estate, the widow grew bitter and quarrelsome. Her conduct was censured by the church. Neighbors accused her of being a witch, and a jury found her guilty, but the General Court reversed its decision. Yet public clamor against her grew so loud that the Court condemned her to death. Thomas Hutchinson commented:

> It fared with her as it did with Joan of Arc in France. Some counted her a saint and some a witch, and some observed solemn marks of Providence set upon those who were very forward to condemn her and to brand others upon the like ground with the like reproach. This was the second instance of any person's being executed for witchcraft in New England.

The Salem Witchcraft Trials

A witchcraft scare of major proportions began in Salem early in 1692. Accusations were brought against more than 200 people, and 150 were arrested and imprisoned. A special court was convened. William Stoughton, deputy-governor of Massachusetts presided. The other judges were John Hawthorne (ancestor of Nathaniel Hawthorne), John Corwin, John Higginson, and, though he was present at only one trial, Samuel Sewall. They examined the accused and passed judgment. As a result of their deliberations twenty innocent people were executed. Thirteen women and six men were hanged. Because he refused to plead, one man, Giles Corey, was slowly pressed to death.

The uproar over the loss of the charter, the antagonism toward the governing British, the consequent anger and bitterness had affected people's minds and emotions. Rational judgment was in abeyance. As they do at any time, the spirit of discontent and anarchy abroad provoked senseless outbursts. People were looking for someone to blame for their misery and exulted when they found usable scapegoats. More than the maliciousness of some undisciplined teenage girls was responsible for what happened in Salem in 1692.

The trouble began in the home of the Rev. Samuel Parris in Salem Village (Danvers). In continual dispute with the church to which he had come only three years earlier, Parris had been in business in the West Indies and brought with him to Massachusetts as servants a West Indian woman and her husband.

A number of young girls aged nine to twenty were in the habit of gathering in the Parris home. Some of them began to show alarming symptoms of an epileptic nature. Tibuta, the Indian woman, claimed she could exorcise evil spirits and tried to cast out those which were supposedly tormenting the girls. Whether as a result of her suggestions or from genuine hysterical illness or from a desire to attract attention, the girls soon began to show the classic symptoms of being bewitched. They writhed in torment; they were seized with fits. They cried out that they were being pinched and pulled by invisible hands. They drew back their tongues until they nearly choked, or let them loll to their chins. They were first struck deaf, then dumb. Dumbness forgotten, they screamed that they were being burned or cut by unseen knives.

Twelve-year old Anne Putnam showed the most virulent afflictions. Her mother joined with her in accusing not only Tibuta but also two aged and highly respected women of the community, Martha Corey and Rebecca Nurse. The contagion spread. Everyone knew that witchcraft was the work of the devil, and the devil was as familiar as God or the minister. If a child was epileptic or idiotic,

Preliminary examinations for those accused of witchcraft were held at the home of Jonathan Corwin, judge of the Witchcraft Court. Now restored, it is known as the Witch House

Cotton Mather was scientist, historian, and community leader as well as the last of the Mather dynasty

if you caught a fever or met with misfortune, it was the work of the devil carried out by his willing assistants—the witches who made compacts with him in secret night meetings in the woods and fields. It was the duty of all God-fearing people to ferret them out for torture and death.

It was also a magnificent opportunity to work off old grudges. Neighbors accused neighbors they disliked. Servants accused masters and mistresses, and they in turn accused their servants. Bewildered small children, perhaps angry at being punished for some offense, accused their mothers. The judges listened as seriously to the prattlings of these children as to the honest or malignant testimony of their elders.

Conducted by conscientious men who were as superstitious as their fellows, the trials were less investigations than inquisitions. They violated the fundamental principles of Anglo-Saxon law. Those accused were presumed to be guilty. There were juries, but they merely acquiesced in the verdicts of the judges. The defendants were allowed no counsel nor were they allowed to speak in their own defense. All the terrified prisoners could do was declare and reiterate their innocence.

Fifty-five men and women confessed to being witches either out of panic or the hope that after confession they would be set free. Some were, but hysteria was so widespread that little helped. The Putnams, the Rev. Samuel Parris, and the Rev. Nicholas Noyes of Salem were indefatigible in seeking out suspects and having them brought to trial. Young Cotton Mather, already the most powerful minister in Massachusetts, whipped popular excitement to a frenzy with his fired belief in witchcraft. He even defended the sentence at the foot of the scaffold when some of the crowd objected to the hanging of the Rev. George Burroughs. Burroughs was hanged together with John Willard, John Procter, Martha Carrier, and George Jacobs on Gallows Hill in Salem on August 19, 1692.

The madness grew madder. The wife of the Rev. John Hale of Beverly, a Mather relative, was accused. The Rev. Samuel Willard of the Old South Church in Boston was accused. Because of her known sympathy with the victims and her distaste for executions, the cry went up that the wife of Governor Phips was a witch. This brought an abrupt end to the Salem Witchcraft trials. Phips, who had been out of the colony while the trials were going on, ordered an end to them.

Reaction was immediate. The girls whose accusations had brought violent death to twenty innocent people and the imprisonment of small children as well as their parents under vile conditions, who had ruined the lives of hundreds, were discredited. The jury repented. Individuals who had been active in the persecution acknowledged their error. The Salem church struck from its records the sentences of excommunication passed against those executed. None of this brought back the dead.

In 1767, Governor Thomas Hutchinson summed it all up this way:

The opinion which prevailed in New England for many years after this tragedy, that there was something preternatural in it, and that it was not all the effect of fraud and imposture, proceeded from the reluctance in human nature to reject errors once

Salem from the lookout on Witches Hill, where those who were executed for witchcraft were buried

imbibed. . . . A little attention must force the conclusion that the whole was a scene of fraud and imposture, begun by young girls, who at first thought of nothing more than being pitied and indulged, and continued by adult persons who were afraid of being accused themselves. The one and the other, rather than confess their fraud, suffered the lives of so many innocents to be taken away, through the credulity of judges and juries.

The twentieth century is accustomed to the deaths of millions in global wars and to the methodical perpetration of mass atrocities. Violence, murder, and assassination have become commonplace in American cities. Contemporary United States is hardly in a position to condemn the Massachusetts colonists for the sadistic orgy in Salem in 1692. Yet horror persists at the indignities, pain, and death which irresponsible girls and deluded but self-righteous men and women inflicted on helpless victims almost three hundred years ago.

CHAPTER EIGHT

The Great Awakening

Royal governor followed royal governor in the Province of Massachusetts Bay. Some were Massachusetts men appointed by the crown; others were sent from England. Each had his entourage of royal appointees, British regular troops under his command, and a British frigate or two in the harbor.

There were the capable and the less capable among these men. Some were hated, others tolerated. Politics then, as politics at any time, was fierce and devious. Men tried to manipulate the machinery of government for their own ends. Because to do so would be to acknowledge their authority, Massachusetts refused to pay the royal governors a regular salary. The province made gifts, often large gifts, of funds for the support of the governor and his aides but would not meet an obligation which had not been levied by Massachusetts.

French and Indian Wars

Just as governor followed governor, war followed war. With the other New England colonies, Massachusetts fought the French and their Indian allies for England and her own survival. These long and bloody wars in which England fought to take Canada and the west from France began in 1690 and continued until 1760, when the British took Montreal.

The long conflict was broken into King William's War, 1690 to 1697, when Massachusetts troops under Sir William Phips took Port Royal in Nova Scotia but failed to capture Quebec; Queen Anne's

War, 1701 to 1713, which resulted in the deportation of the Acadians from Nova Scotia; and King George's War, 1745 to 1748, which saw the siege and capture of Louisburg by colonial troops under Sir William Pepperell. Pepperell, who had been Chief Justice of Massachusetts and a lieutenant-general, was knighted and made *de facto* governor in 1756 for his military achievements.

According to Thomas Hutchinson, between five and six thousand young men died in Indian wars between 1675 and 1713. The siege of Louisburg cost another two or three thousand. Once more towns were raided and burned. Men were struck down in their fields by marauding Indians, and women and children were enslaved and carted off to Canada. Though there were raids farther east, it was the Connecticut Valley towns which suffered most. Their inhabitants lived in a constant state of alarm. The militia was almost continually active, and there were high bounties on Indian scalps.

Deerfield was laid waste once more. Outfitted in Canada, a war party of three hundred French and Indians, struck in deep snow the night of February 29, 1704. They fired the town and killed many of its people. Their minister, the Rev. John Williams, who had warned of the danger of imminent attack, faced an Indian who broke into his house, but his pistol misfired. The Indians murdered two of his children and a Negro woman of the household.

Williams, his wife, and their five remaining children were enslaved as were the other survivors of the attack. The Indians dragged their captives through the harsh New England winter on a forced march to Canada. When Mrs. Williams could not keep up, her Indian master sunk his tomahawk in her skull. Twenty more of the captives died in the snow and cold before reaching Canada.

Those who came through the ordeal alive were kindly treated by the French in Canada, who made every effort to convert them to Roman Catholicism. Governor Dudley managed to get John Williams released, and he returned to Boston with the story he told later in *The Redeemed Captive Returning to Zion, 1707.*

The Indian House Memorial in Deerfield is a reproduction of the house which received the brunt of the French and Indian attack in 1704. Inside, visitors may see some paraphernalia of a colonial kitchen

The Rev. Solomon Stoddard

Another minister was the most powerful religious and political force in the Connecticut Valley during these years. Tall and formidable, admired and feared by his parishioners, Solomon Stoddard was the minister of Northhampton for the sixty years from 1670 to 1729. The Indians called him "the white man's god." He was known throughout the Valley as "the pope of Hampshire." Solomon Stoddard was squire as well as minister in Northampton. He lived in and ruled from the great mansion he built for his manse in 1684. It still stands imposing and well kept near the campus of Smith College.

Stoddard was famous throughout Massachusetts for his church policy. In 1662, a synod meeting at Cambridge had adopted the famous Half-Way Covenant. Under its terms an applicant could be admitted to church membership if he were of good moral life and subscribed to church doctrine even if he could not submit convincing evidence of having undergone religious conversion. Because they were not "Visible Saints," these members could not partake of Communion, but they could have their children baptized. This was important as the Puritans believed that, because of man's fall from grace, unbaptized infants were condemned to hell and eternal torment.

Solomon Stoddard went even further than the compromise of the Half-Way Covenant. Under a practice which became known as Stoddardeanism, he admitted people to full church membership, including Communion, without their having to produce proof of having been "saved." Stoddard required only a profession of faith and repentance for sins. He considered Communion itself a means of regeneration. Through his leadership this practice was adopted throughout western Massachusetts.

Stoddard was succeeded as squire of Northampton by his son Colonel John Stoddard. Representative of the crown in western Massachusetts, commander of all its armed forces, his voice heeded in the councils of the province in Boston, he ruled from the manse, which he enlarged.

Solomon Stoddard was succeeded as Northampton's minister by his grandson.

Jonathan Edwards

A graduate of Yale in 1720 and, as senior tutor, virtually in charge of the college from 1722 to 1725, Jonathan Edwards was twenty-three years old when he became his maternal grandfather's assistant in 1726. He was twenty-six when he took over the largest church in Massachusetts outside of Boston. ⌐

Edwards was a mystic and a scholar. His was the finest abstract intelligence produced in the American colonies, perhaps the finest in all American history. His theological and philosophic works, including the famous *Freedom of the Will* are classics of American thought and writing. Tall, thin, austere, his inner life enriched by his deep consciousness of God, his outward manner marked by dig-

Jonathan Edwards

nity and reserve, Edwards first became known throughout New England and abroad for quite something else.

Religion mattered intensely in the Connecticut Valley. People worked hard, drank hard, and fought hard. Church on Sunday was an important part of their lives. Red-coated farmers in their checked shirts galloped to church at the sound of the drum, later the ringing of the bell, their strong wives riding pillion behind them. Their children shouted and played, threw stones and sometimes broke windows, as families picnicked about the church between morning and afternoon services in good weather.

Solomon Stoddard admitted 630 new members to the Northampton church, most of them during revivals which he called his "times of harvest." Jonathan Edwards was expected to follow his grandfather's example. He believed that religion was basically a thing not of the mind but of the emotions. His own deep religious experiences and those of his beautiful young wife had convinced him of the validity of what were then called the "religious affections." Edwards was a compelling preacher, and he exhorted his people to revivalistic excitement. During the first "awakening" under his Northampton ministry in 1734 and 1735 there were more than three hundred conversions in six months.

Edwards fired not only Northampton, but also, from contagion, Hadley, South Hadley, Hatfield, Deerfield, Long Meadow, and the Connecticut towns of Suffield and Enfield. The young stopped going to parties and held religious socials instead. Older people were carried away with religious ecstacy; even young children were affected.

As Edwards wrote Dr. Benjamin Colman, liberal pastor of Boston's Brattle Street church, ". . . a great and earnest concern, about the things of religion and the eternal world became universal in all parts of the town, and among persons of all degrees and all ages. . . . All other talk but about spiritual and eternal things was soon thrown by. . . . Religion was with all sorts the great concern, and the world was a thing only by the way." Colman had Edwards' remarkable

George Whitefield, the celebrated divine. "This extraordinary man journeyed over England, Scotland, and America. His preaching was attended with astonishing effects, and when the churches were shut against him, he gathered immence congregations in the open air"

account printed as *A Faithful Narrative* . . . and circulated in England as well as in Massachusetts.

George Whitefield

Born in 1714, George Whitefield was an English evangelist who drew crowds of ten and even twenty thousand people in England with his hypnotic preaching. He was an actor and an orator who affected scholars and miners, scientists, statesmen, and farm laborers. When he came to the colonies in 1739, he moved even Benjamin Franklin, who estimated the crowd to which Whitefield preached on the Philadelphia streets at thirty thousand. Whitefield preached his way up the coast. When he neared Boston, a son of Governor Belcher and a party of ministers and gentlemen rode four miles out of the city to greet him. Enthusiastic crowds heard Whitefield in the Brattle Street church, on Boston Common, and in the Harvard Yard. When he left Boston, Governor Belcher himself took him in his coach on the ferry across the Charles River, wept, and kissed him goodbye.

After preaching in Worcester, Hadley, and other towns, White-field came to Northampton where he was a house guest of the Edwardses. The Northampton congregation moaned and screamed for joy when he preached. The brilliant, analytical, but sensitive Jonathan Edwards wept all through the service. There were no horse-drawn vehicles in western Massachusetts. Edwards rode horseback with Whitefield as far as his father's home in Windsor, Connecticut, which was the next stop on the evangelist's itinerary.

Only twenty-six years old at the time, George Whitefield inflamed New England, and Jonathan Edwards became the leader of the new revival for which he had been praying.

The Awakening of 1740

This was the "Great Awakening" which raged like a fire throughout Massachusetts. Backed at first by the liberal clergy in Boston, it was accepted everywhere, sweeping through town after town and church after church, tossing people to new heights of religious abandon. People wept and fainted, fell into fits, shouted for the glory of God and the excitement of it all.

Edwards among them, groups of ministers rode from town to town exhorting. It was when the Great Awakening was at its height that he delivered his "Sermon Preached at Enfield," better known as "Sinners in the Hands of an Angry God," for which posterity has unjustly vilified him. Edwards believed that the Great Awakening was a visitation of God's spirit. Because it was seated in the emotions, he believed this true religion, but he worried that some shrieked and contorted themselves only out of a desire to outdo their fellows. He warned against false demonstrations. He tried to help people distinguish between true and false symptoms of conversion, but he was too late.

The Great Awakening got out of hand. Bands of lay exhorters, some of them not quite sane, took it upon themselves to invade churches and urge people hysterically to forsake their godless and

unconverted ministers and follow them. There were revivalistic celebrations that became sensual orgies. The "New Lights," as the fol-
lowers of revivalism were called, ranted and wrote pamphlets against
the conservative "Old Lights," who retaliated in kind.

Rich and poor, educated and ignorant had thrown themselves into
the Great Awakening, but its excesses began to disturb not only important conservative ministers who had detested it from the start,
but also the liberals, such as Benjamin Colman, who had supported
it. They withdrew their approval. The Great Awakening had spent
its force. In Northampton, as elsewhere, some would have kept it
going for the excitement of it, but the majority turned against it.
The Great Awakening spread to other colonies, particularly in the
South, where it lasted until about 1750, but in Massachusetts it declined swiftly after about three years' time.

When George Whitefield returned to Boston in 1744 he was not
welcomed as he had been earlier. Ministerial bodies drew up petitions
against him. Harvard, whose piety he had attacked, accused him of
wicked and libelous falsehood. Whitefield retained a strong following
among the common people, but he had lost his hold on the influential and the thoughtful. The Great Awakening fell into disrepute
and Jonathan Edwards, who had been its hero, was left its defender
and in many ways its victim.

Dismissal of Edwards

An intellectual aristocrat and a poetic mystic, Edwards had mingled socially only with the elite of Northampton. He had awakened
resentments in a particularly quarrelsome town. He had made enemies of two families of his relatives, the Hawleys and the wealthy
and powerful Williams family of Hatfield.

Edwards made matters worse in a series of sermons designed to distinguish between true and suspect religious emotions. Many who had
most gloried in their conversions felt he was saying that they were
not truly saved. He then took what to Northampton townspeople

seemed an indefensible and traitorous stand. He went back on Stoddardeanism. He went back on the Half-Way Covenant itself. Edwards now insisted that every applicant for membership in the Northampton church present public proof of having undergone a regenerating religious experience. His parish was horrified. A bitter quarrel broke out between minister and congregation.

Edwards had also tactlessly made enemies among the Hampshire county clergy who were welded in a strong organization. When the quarrel was brought before them for adjudication, they decided against him. By a vote of ten to nine they declared for his dismissal. Egged on by his cousin, Joseph Hawley, and by Major Seth Pomeroy, the congregation accepted the clerical verdict. More than 230 of the male members of the Northampton congregation voted to cast out Jonathan Edwards.

A year later, Edwards went to the backwoods village of Stockbridge in the Berkshires to be both minister to the small church there and missionary to several hundred Indians. (With Edwards present in the manse during discussions among clergy and politicians, Solomon Stoddard had been instrumental in establishing the mission there.)

It was during the seven years he spent in Stockbridge on the extreme western border of Massachusetts that Edwards wrote his great books. He had just assumed the presidency of Princeton (then called the College of New Jersey) when he died, March 22, 1758, of an inoculation for smallpox.

CHAPTER NINE

Mid-Eighteenth-Century Massachusetts

One hundred years and more after the founding of the colony, the Puritan church, its tenets and its ethics, still prevailed in Massachusetts. Anti-Puritan beliefs and behavior were also strong.

Over the century, newcomers to whom the Calvinism of Winthrop, Cotton, Brewster, and Bradford meant nothing had infiltrated the colony. Descendants of the original settlers paid more attention to this life than to the next. King's Chapel was built in Boston in 1684 so that the provincial governor and his entourage could have their own place of worship. Thus the very Church of England which the Puritans had fled came to the Holy Commonwealth. The present King's Chapel in Boston—it became Unitarian after the Revolution—was built in 1754. By that time Baptists and Quakers, the heretics who had been whipped out of Massachusetts Bay, had their own meeting houses there.

Boston

Mid-eighteenth-century travelers saw Boston as a busy seaport and a flourishing English city. The harbor was filled with English and Massachusetts ships. The fisheries and shipyards employed thousands. Rum, tea, spices, sugar, molasses, English hardware, and American lumber were piled up on the wharves that jutted into the Bay.

The Town Watch policed cobbled streets and paved walks. Massachusetts ships brought back the luxuries of Europe, even treasures from the Orient. Boston had brick buildings and tall churches.

A VIEW OF PART OF THE TOWN OF BOSTON IN NEW ENGLAND AND BRITISH SHIPS OF WAR LANDING THEIR TROOPS. 1768

British troops kept formal guard mount at Province House, a three-story brick mansion on spacious grounds. Boston had a population of about 25,000 people, and it had some three thousand homes. Among them the town houses of the wealthy shone with polished silver and furniture, and oil portraits gleamed on paneled walls. The rich and well placed rode in their coaches. They had many servants and perhaps an Indian or African slave or two. Beaux and belles paraded the London fashions about Boston Common.

Mansion interiors displayed eighteenth-century elegance and charm. Some of the finest cabinet work was imported from England; some of it was fashioned by American craftsmen after English models. There were graceful chairs, handsome tables, carved chests, chests-on-chests, highboys, lowboys, silver candelabra. There were slant-top desks, plain, curved, or block-fronted. There were Winthrop desks and delicate-appearing but strongly made Windsor chairs. Brass hardware and candlesticks struck light on polished walnut, mahogany, and burled maple.

The governing class and the mercantile aristocracy lived well in the most important city in North America, a center of trade, finance, and education. Boston Latin and Harvard were both over one hundred years old. Boston already had its traditions.

There were even romances, one of them famous. Greatly respected Chief Justice of Massachusetts, Samuel Sewall was a man of honor and courage. Alone of the Salem witchcraft judges, he made public confession of his guilt in the Old South Church and asked God's forgiveness for his error. Three times married and the father of fourteen children, he began to court a widow, Madame Winthrop, when he was 68. He pressed his suit with gifts of sermons, gingerbread, and sugared almonds. For a time he seemed to be doing well, but the lady thought the marriage settlement he offered too little and wanted.

Paul Revere gave a good idea of Boston's colonial urbanization—its growing population and number of homes—in his engraving of the port of Boston, 1768, with British ships of war landing their troops

him to keep a coach. There were other differences. Sewall noted the ups and down of his courtship in his diary and then recorded its end.

> . . . Gave her the remnants of my almonds; She did not eat of them as before; but laid them away; I said I came to enquire whether she had alter'd her mind since Friday, or remained of the same mind still. She said, Thereabouts. I told her I loved her and was so fond as to think she loved me; she said she had a great respect for me. . . . The fire was come to one short brand besides the block, which brand was set up on end; at last it fell to pieces, and no recruit was made; she gave me a glass of wine. I think I repeated again that I would go home and bewail my rashness in making more haste than good speed. I would endeavor to contain myself, and not to go on to solicit her to do that which she could not consent to. Took leave of her. As came down the steps she bid me have a care. Treated me courteously. Told her she had entered the 4th year of her widowhood. I had given her the News-Letter before: I did not bid her draw off her glove [to kiss her hand] as sometimes I had done. Her dress was not so clean as sometime it had been. Jehovah jireh!

Eight days before his seventieth birthday Samuel Sewall married Mrs. May Gibbs, a Newtown widow.

The Towns

A large and prosperous class of mechanics and tradesmen lived well too. Their homes were substantial and comfortable. Pewter dishes predominated. Furniture, if not as fine, was soundly built and pleasant to look at. In the farming towns—and except on the coast all towns were farming towns—there was usually a mansion or two, then large and comfortable village homes. Maple and fruit woods, some pine, were used for furniture in ordinary homes, though a piece or two may have been brought from England or purchased in Boston.

In the Connecticut Valley, people raised their own food and spun, wove, and even dyed their own cloth. Game was plentiful. The price of venison in Northampton was about twopence a pound. Everyone had salt pork. Wild pigeons flew over in such clouds that they could be taken in nets. People could not eat all they caught. After plucking the feathers for beds and pillows, they fed the pigeons to their pigs. In spring, the Connecticut teemed with huge shad; it was easy to catch thirty or forty in a day. The river also provided great salmon, which people ate fresh or salted for the winter.

Wolves were always a danger. Between 1700 and 1730 Massachusetts paid bounties to hunters for killing over 2,800 wolves. Farmers mingled work and drink with the excitements of religious revivals, roistering at weddings, church attendance, and tormenting old women suspected of being witches. They drilled on training days, and, if a man were lucky, he might get one hundred pounds for an Indian scalp in 1745.

Dress and Customs

Most men in the Valley towns wore their own hair. Gentlemen, and in Boston many men of all classes, wore wigs. Men of fashion wore large custom-made periwigs with their silk stockings, satin breeches, velvet coats, and embroidered waistcoats. Wigs got smaller toward the mid-century: tye wigs, bag wigs, bob wigs. At home, men took off the wigs and wore silk turbans on their shaved heads.

Fashionable women wore wigs from about 1760 to 1780. At home they wore mob caps. Men and women who did not wear wigs wore their hair long. They dressed and powdered it and tied it back with a black or colored ribbon so that it would look as much as possible like a wig.

Women often died young. They married early and families of ten to fifteen children were not unusual. Yet there were widows as well as widowers, and most remarried. Second and third marriages were general. From the beginning, marriage was a civil contract in Massachusetts, performed by magistrates. Later they were also performed by ministers but as civil, not religious, ceremonies. Even divorce was possible by the mid-century. The governor and his council, sitting as a court, heard thirty-six divorce cases in Massachusetts between 1760 and 1774.

Work and Play

Maritime trade was Boston's big business. Wealth made successful merchants the social equals of the governing British and the clergy. Smaller entrepreneurs kept store. There were shops of many kinds in Boston, some making furniture, clothing, silverware, saddlery, and the like on order, for they were manufacturers as well as distributors. Other shops merely bought at wholesale and sold at retail, both imported and domestic goods. Men were killed in wars or accidents or died early of disease. Often their widows kept on their shops, the printing business, the tavern, or whatever other enterprise they had helped their husbands run.

The trades flourished. All of those connected with the sea had their apprentices, journeymen, and master craftsmen. Trades connected with the home were as busy. Boston had its carpenters, joiners, masons, painters, braziers, plumbers, upholsterers. The barbers were always busy, as were the wigmakers. Saddlers, clothiers, pewterers, and smiths in iron, gold, or silver plied their skills. The artisan class was one of substance and standing in busy Boston.

Like most cities, Boston had its great fires. Most houses were of wood. Warehouses as well as houses, even ships at dock, went up in flames during a fire in 1679, when the Mathers lost both their home and their church. The fire of 1711 was in the very center of the city. It burned all the houses on both sides of Cornhill Street down to Dock Square, all those on both sides of King (now State) Street, and destroyed the Town House, which had to be rebuilt. There were disastrous fires also in 1690, 1747, and 1760.

Each time Boston was rebuilt. Whether induced by disaster, necessity, or habit, work was inbred in the Boston temperament. Idleness was still a sin, but play had crept in.

There were football games, and boys kicked footballs about enough so that windows were often broken. There was horse racing. There were traveling menageries and performances by trained animals. Massachusetts had few holidays, but there were many occasions for diverting celebrations.

The king's or queen's birthday meant cannon salutes and martial music, bonfires, and parades. The arrival of a new governor meant more cannon fire, illuminations, formal receptions at Province House, and ceremonies at the Town House. Christmas was ignored, but Thanksgiving meant feasting and socializing. Election day—election of men to the governor's council—was celebrated with parades and excitement. Spring and fall training days were great public spectacles, with booths set up for the entertainment and refreshment of the populace. The Ancient and Honorable Artillery Company was an elite body already more than a century old. It had its own annual election day to choose its officers, and the Artillery Sermon was preached the preceding Sunday. To give this sermon was an honor for any clergyman; in the early nineteenth century Ralph Waldo Emerson's father was its chaplain. The Company still conducts its annual ceremonies.

Harvard's Commencement was another annual festival. It was not then a severely academic ceremony but a great public celebration with the revelry continuing for a week. All of these occasions were

Woodcut of a schoolroom scene from *The Juvenile Biographer, Containing the Lives of Little Masters and Misses*, published in Worcester in 1787

signalized by even more drinking than usual. The Massachusetts colonists drank even harder than the English at home, and they drank deeply and continually. The wealthy drank toast after toast in choice Madeira at dinner parties and sipped or tossed down their rum punch. Taverns patterned after the English ordinaries were the gathering places where other men drank and, though there were laws forbidding it, diced and played cards. The laws forbidding the use of tobacco had long since been repealed. The wealthy had their dances and, in winter, their sleighing parties. Ordinary people had their frivolities too. In 1747, one Thomas Clagget, a clockmaker shot sparks from person to person in a demonstration of "The Wonderful Phenomena of Electrical Attraction, Repulsion, and Flamific Force."

As in England, executions were popular with all classes. Hangings drew crowds of thrilled thousands. Death has always awed and attracted. Even ordinary funerals were made occasions of feasting and drinking, and the funerals of prominent men became more and more elaborate.

Burial expenses were often so heavy that men provided for them in their wills. It was the custom to give gold rings and white gloves to officiating ministers, close relatives, family intimates, and pall bearers. When the wealthy Huguenot merchant, Andrew Faneuil, died in 1738, two hundred rings and three thousand pairs of gloves were given away. A Boston minister of the time reported that he got about fifteen pounds worth of rings and gloves every year. When Governor William Burnet died in 1729 almost eleven hundred pounds was drawn from the public treasury to pay for his funeral expenses.

Newspapers

Founded in 1704, the *Boston News-Letter* got its local news from many sources and reprinted the foreign news, often months late, from the English newspapers. The first issue printed solicited advertising at rates of from twelve pence to one shilling. Advertisements often tell more about the people of a time and how they lived than the news, and there were three in this first issue. One offered a fulling mill for sale or for lease. The other two offered rewards for the capture of thieves. One (evidently the thieves were muscular) read:

> Lost on the 10th of April last off Mr. Shippens Wharf in Boston, Two Iron Anvils, weighing between 120-140 pounds each; Whoever has taken them up, and will bring or give true intelligence of them to John Campbell, Postmaster, shall have a sufficient reward.

The *Boston Gazette,* founded in 1719, was printed by James Franklin, who had learned his trade in England and brought a press and type back to Boston. When he lost the printing to a competitor, Franklin started his own *New England Courant,* its first issue appearing August 7, 1721. Imitating Addison and Steele in the *Spectator,* Franklin wrote flippantly of both church and state in Massachusetts, shocking Cotton Mather. He ridiculed experiments in inoculating for smallpox. When he accused the authorities of laxity in dealing with pirates, Franklin was jailed for a month. After he printed unpleasant remarks about church members, he was forbidden to publish his paper. Thereupon, beginning in February 1723, the *Courant* was published in the name of James's half-brother, apprentice, and impudent contributor, Benjamin Franklin.

Born in Boston in 1706, Benjamin Franklin had gone to work at ten years of age as an assistant to his father, a tallow chandler. He had been apprenticed as a printer when he was twelve. The newspaper continually carried advertising for the return of runaway slaves, servants, and apprentices. On September 30, 1723, the *Courant* advertised for a "like lad for an Apprentice." Though no other advertisement offered a reward for his return, Benjamin Franklin had run away to Philadelphia.

The son of a French Huguenot father who had changed his name from Apollos DeRevoire was a fine silversmith who also made and sold false teeth. In a *Boston Gazette* advertisement, December 19, 1768, Paul Revere claimed that the teeth he made looked as well as natural teeth and were an aid in speaking. He neglected to say whether or not they would be useful in eating.

The Boston town clerk, Ezekiel Goldthwaite, flailed indignantly at unfair competition in an advertisement in the *Gazette*, February 13, 1760. He fulminated against "sundry evil minded Persons in some of the neighboring Townes" who had started rumors that smallpox raged in Boston. There had been but one case that year.

The idea of ingenious suburban merchants was to discourage farmers from bringing their produce to the Boston market. Instead, they bought them up cheaply, took them into Boston themselves, and sold them at exorbitant prices. Mr. Goldthwaite warned the miscreants that they were known to the Boston selectmen and that, unless they stopped their lying, they would be prosecuted. A postscript to his advertisement throws light on one of the many symbols of the day.

> Many Country-People have imagined by seeing Silks hanging on Poles, that the Small-pox is in such Houses, but their Surmises are entirely groundless, they being hung out at the Silk Dyers for drying.

An advertiser in the *Gazette,* September 22, 1667, listed the articles he would take in exchange for New England rum. They included Barbados rum, sugar, Bohea tea, flour, indigo, pitch, tar, cordage, sole leather, English steel, and "Dumb FISH."

An angry and worried Richard Silvester at the Sign of the Broken Post gave solemn warning in the *Boston Chronicle* when, March 1, 1770, he demanded the return of his black and white horse.

> The persons concerned in this Frolick, who were seen and known, are desired to replace the said Horse, in the manner and form they found him. And it is hoped, as it is hoped, as he is a young creature, they will not corrupt his morals by teaching him any of their tricks. . . .

Books

Printers turned themselves into editors and publishers in the Province of Massachusetts. They issued not only newspapers but books as well. Classics, religious books, and the latest English literature—Richardson, Fielding, Sterne, Smollett, and Pope, who was a favorite—were all imported from England, but Massachusetts published sermons, tracts, Psalm books, almanacs, and texts.

Many people could not read, which is why shops and taverns were designated by signs and symbols; but if a man was illiterate in Massachusetts, it was his own fault or that of his parents. Schools had been provided from the earliest years of the colony. Girls were taught at home, but boys learned their letters in dame or "ma'am" schools. Children were taught from hornbooks—a paddle on which a sheet of parchment, with the Lord's Prayer, the alphabet, and sometimes a moral or two printed on it, was fastened under a covering of transparent horn.

Common schools taught reading, writing, and ciphering. All towns

One of the first educational tools, the hornbook appeared in England during the sixteenth century and came to America with the settlers

did not maintain the grammar schools which the law ordered, but most did the best they could. In Boston, Boston Latin had its seven-year curriculum based on the classics.

Many clergymen and other educated men had libraries of hundreds, sometimes even thousands, of books. Almost every household had at least three books: a Bible, an almanac, and a *New England Primer*. Printer competing against printer, there were many almanacs with their calendars, dates, phases of the moon, jokes, and proverbs, but there was only one *New England Primer*.

It was first published, somewhere between 1683 and 1690, by the Boston bookseller, Benjamin Harris. It came out in edition after edition with changes and additions. Called "the little Bible of New England," it was the most widely read and studied book in Massachusetts for more than a century.

In all, some five million copies of what must have been America's original best-seller are said to have been sold. *The New England Primer* contained the letters of the alphabet in rhymes, moral texts, prayers, and religious verse. It was meant to teach reading, writing, and Puritan morality all at the same time.

A In *Adam's* Fall
We finned all.

B Thy Life to mend
This Book attend.

C The Cat doth play
And after flay.

D A Dog will bite
A Thief at Nig

E The Eagle's Fli
Is out of Sight.

F The idle Fool
Is whipt at Scho

First page of the *New England Primer*

CHAPTER TEN

Revolution and the
Commonwealth of Massachusetts

The American Revolution did not come on suddenly. In a sense, it began when the Pilgrims and then the Puritans first came to Massachusetts. From the viewpoint of many in England they were heretics and eccentric malcontents. England was well rid of them. From their own viewpoint and that of their descendants they were free and independent spirits, men of strong convictions and intent. They meant to have their own way in governing the communities they established and in the practical business of day-to-day living.

From the first, they would tolerate no interference from any quarter. They besieged England for every favor they could obtain and some which they could not, but they would bear no restrictions and bow to no demands. The Province of Massachusetts Bay gave surface compliance to England's royal governors, but underneath, and not very far underneath, there was resentment. Massachusetts had once ruled itself. Its charter had been wrung from it. It never forgave the injury.

England was likewise resentful. Not unjustly, she was determined that her American colonies help defray the expense of governing them, especially the costs of wars and the armed forces she had to maintain in America for the protection of the colonists. England was particularly bitter that, flouting all existing laws, Boston had traded profitably with the enemy during the French and Indian wars and that Massachusetts had profiteered in selling produce and supplies to the British troops.

The immediate causes of unrest were a series of unwise actions by the colonial authorities in England. They began fifteen years before the outbreak of the Revolution in Massachusetts. In chronological order the actions were: the Writs of Assistance under which customs officers could search homes and business places for smuggled merchandise, 1761; the Stamp Act, a tax of a few shillings to several pounds on newspapers, diplomas, deeds, and all legal documents, 1765; the Townshend Act, which placed heavy duties on most goods imported by the colonies, 1767; the tax on tea, retained after repeal of the Townshend Act, 1770; the punitive closing of the port of Boston, 1774.

As potent a cause of the Revolution as England's actions were the machinations of Massachusetts politicians disputing among themselves out of moral principle, political convictions—and personal hatred.

Intent on maintaining or advancing their own fortunes, at the same time seeking revenge for real or fancied slights, two politicians made capital out of attacking English rule. Another, the most powerful figure in Massachusetts, staunchly defended his own position and the sanctity and authority of Britain. A fourth man—legalistic, moral, humorless—argued and fought for what seemed to him just and reasonable.

An artist's conception of the flight of Hutchinson before the rioters in 1765

The men were James Otis, Samuel Adams, Thomas Hutchinson, and John Adams.

All of them came of Old Massachusetts families. Their forebears had held important colonial offices or been prominent in their communities. All of them were Harvard men. Thomas Hutchinson graduated in 1727, took his M.A. in 1730; Samuel Adams took his B.A. in 1740; his M.A. in 1743; James Otis graduated in 1743; and John Adams graduated in 1755. There the similarities among the four men ceased.

Thomas Hutchinson

Born in Boston in 1711, Governor Thomas Hutchinson came of a wealthy family. His grandfather had been both a judge and a member of the Council. His father, a prosperous merchant, was a member of the Council. Even as a Harvard undergraduate, Thomas Hutchinson made money by taking ventures in his father's ships. By the time he was twenty-one he was part owner of a ship himself. A scholar, Hutchinson knew Greek, Latin, and French and was deeply interested in Massachusetts history.

Hutchinson entered politics in 1737 when he became both a selectman of Boston and a member of the House of Representatives in the General Court, where he served for eleven years, three of them as Speaker. Massachusetts sent him on a mission to England in 1740. He served in the Council from 1747 to 1766, was made lieutenant-governor in 1758 and chief justice in 1760. An advocate of hard money, Hutchinson managed to stabilize the currency of Massachusetts; in 1764, he went to England to protest the imposition of duties on sugar—and, incidentally, to get the second volume of his history of Massachusetts published in London.

Careful in the management of his business and financial interests, devoted to his family, Hutchinson was a man of the highest integrity. Although he opposed many of the restrictive measures adopted by Britain to control her colonies, he thought it his duty to enforce them. He was unswerving in his loyalty to the crown. Thomas Hutchinson was made governor—the last royal governor of Massachusetts—in 1771.

Hutchinson was a traditionalist and a high Tory. Despite much American romantic historical fiction, the Tories were not necessarily wicked and the Whigs virtuous. Whig and Tory were simply the names of opposing political parties in England. The Tories were the conservatives; in general, they were the aristocrats. In Massachusetts the Tories were Loyalists. The Whig party in England was the liberal party. The Whigs were the "outs" in the 1760s; the Tories were the "ins." In the colonies, Whig meant those who opposed British rule. It came to mean those who wished separation from England. This time on political rather than religious grounds, they were Separatists. Later, the Whigs were the "patriots," but at first there was no native country for them to be patriotic about.

James Otis

James Otis studied law after his Harvard graduation, married the daughter of a rich Boston merchant, and began legal practice. Well read, with a quick mind, he was brilliant in the courtroom. Hutchinson himself honestly admitted that he never knew "fairer or more noble conduct in a pleader, than in Otis." The young lawyer became king's advocate in Boston's vice-admiralty court and in 1761 a member of the General Court. At the same time his father, Colonel James Otis, was Speaker of the lower House. They combined forces to oppose Hutchinson and the administration at every point. They had their reasons, or thought they had.

When Chief Justice Samuel Sewall died, the older Otis asked Hutchinson's influence in being appointed an associate justice. Presumably, Hutchinson agreed to do what he could. Instead he accepted the appointment as chief justice himself. This made Hutchinson at the same time a member of the Council, lieutenant-governor, and chief justice. It looked as if he were trying to corner all the profitable offices for himself.

James Otis   John Adams

Colonel Otis felt that Hutchinson had betrayed him. The son felt the same, and is supposed to have declared that he would "set the province in flames, if he perished by the fire."

Otis was a Whig but a moderate. In newspaper articles and in public meetings he demanded only that Massachusetts colonists be granted their rights as Englishmen. In his famous oration of 1761 he spoke against the Writs of Assistance before Hutchinson and the crown lawyers in the assembly room of the Province House. In his impassioned speech of four hours he cried out against "Taxation without Representation."

Almost as well known as Otis's fiery protest itself is John Adam's comment on it. "Otis was a flame of fire! . . . he hurried away everything before him. American independence was then and there born; the seeds of patriots and heroes were then and there sown. . . ."

There was a truce between Thomas Hutchinson and the Otises when, in 1763, Colonel Otis was appointed chief justice of the Court of Common Pleas and probate judge of Barnstable Country where he lived, but the younger James Otis made no truce with his political principles. He enunciated them again in a pamphlet of 1764, "Rights of the British Colonies Asserted and Proved."

> . . . his Majesty George III, is rightful king and sovereign, and
> with his parliament, the supreme legislative of Great Britain,
> France, and Ireland, and the dominions thereunto belonging;

that this constitution is the most free one, and by far the best now existing on earth; that by this constitution every man in the dominions is a free man; that no part of his Majesty's dominions can be taxed without their consent; that every part has a right to be represented in the supreme or some subordinate legislature, that the refusal of this would seem to be a contradiction in practice of the theory of the constitution: and that the colonies are subordinate dominions, and are now in such a state, as to make it best for the good of the whole that they should not only be continued in the enjoyment of subordinate legislation, but be also represented in some proportion to their number and estates in the grand legislation of the nation . . . [was the sum of his argument].

Otis continued to demand traditional civil rights for Massachusetts, but he also continued to uphold England's right to govern. Thus he was infuriated when he discovered that in letters to England he had been branded a malignant incendiary. A brawl with crown officials in a Boston coffeehouse ensued on September 4, 1769. A blow on the head, probably with a cutlass, seemingly affected his mind.

He broke windows in the Province House and fired guns out of a window of his home. John Adams said that in speech he rambled and wandered like a ship without a helm. Adjudged mentally incompetent, he was placed under the guardianship of a younger brother. James Otis was killed by lightning on May 23, 1783.

Samuel Adams

Samuel Adams held a bitter grudge against Thomas Hutchinson too, but there was never anything moderate about Samuel Adams. He was born to wealth and position. His father was a Boston selectman, a justice of the peace, a member of the House, and a deacon of the Old South Church. The family home was one of the finest in Boston. On his father's death, Samuel Adams inherited both the house and his father's prospering brewery. He proved unable to run either one.

Entering local politics, he became Boston's tax collector. He failed at that too, and became technically liable for tax arrears of eight thousand pounds. He ceased trying to support himself and his numerous family.

Impractical, improvident, and irresponsible, Samuel Adams discovered his one great talent in the quarrel between Massachusetts and Great Britain. He became, *par excellence*, the political agitator, the rabble-rousing demagogue. Incapable of logic, he fired the Boston mob to fury by accusing England and its minions with crimes of every kind.

Samuel Adams hated Thomas Hutchinson because the governor's money policy had caused his father considerable financial loss. Adams was out to overthrow Hutchinson as much as he was out to dismiss England. Elected to the House in 1763, he became his party's leader for the next eleven years. He denounced the aristocracy, especially Hutchinson, whom he succeeded in getting out of the Council. He urged on the unruly Sons of Liberty, got the Committee of Correspondence set up in Boston, and wrote a declaration of rights and bill of grievances which he had circulated among the other Massachusetts towns.

Hutchinson had no admiration for this man and is reported to have said, "I doubt whether there is a greater incendiary in the King's dominion or a man of greater malignity of heart."

Many agreed with Thomas Hutchinson, but not Samuel Adams, who knew very well how he was regarded by his enemies. In the *Boston Gazette,* December 7, 1771, signing himself "Candidus," he wrote:

> If the liberties of America are ever completely ruined, of which in my opinion there is now the utmost danger, it will in all probability be the consequence of a mistaken notion of *prudence,* which leads men to acquiesce in measures of the most destructive tendency for the sake of present ease. . . . It has been an old game . . . to hold up the men who would rouse their fellow

Saml Adams

citizens . . . to a sense of their *real* danger . . . as *"pretended patriots," "intemperate politicians," "rash, hot-headed* men," *Incendiaries. . . .*

Adams twisted everything to keep the excitement going and himself a leader. When a lull threatened, he whipped the mob to fury again. He even stooped to using a bigoted religious appeal in his unceasing propaganda.

Samuel Adams was always destructive. Except as the ends he fought for may be thought to justify the means he used, he is difficult to admire. It is almost impossible not to admire his younger cousin.

John Adams

For generations this branch of the Adams family had been substantial farmers in Braintree (once Mount Wollaston, now Quincy), where John Adams was born in 1735. For a time after graduating from Harvard he taught school in Worcester and considered entering the ministry. Instead, he studied law and made an important marriage. Abigail Smith's family was prominent in Massachusetts, and his marriage to her greatly enlarged the young man's acquaintanceship among the influential.

His preparing the resolution for Braintree against the Stamp Act brought Adams into contact with James Otis, and he began to write weekly essays on legal matters as seen from the Whig viewpoint for the *Boston Gazette*. In Boston, he handled important murder and manslaughter cases and defended John Hancock, wealthiest Boston merchant, against smuggling charges.

Adams rose rapidly in the law. Serious, high-principled, he went completely by the book and boasted that he had the only complete set of the British Statutes-at-Large in the American colonies. His Whig sympathies also rose. In his diary for December 18, 1765, he wrote:

> That enormous engine fabricated by the British Parliament, for battering down all the rights and liberties of America, I mean the Stamp Act, has raised and spread through the whole continent a spirit that will be recorded to our honor with all future generations . . . the stamp distributors and inspectors have been compelled by the unconquerable rage of the people to renounce their offices. Such and so universal has been the resentment of the people, that every man who has dared to speak in favor of the stamps or to soften the detestation in which they are held, how great soever his abilities and virtue had been esteemed before, or whatever his fortune, connections or influence had been, has been seen to sink into universal contempt and ignominy.
>
> The people, even to the lowest ranks, have become more attentive to their liberties, more inquisitive about them, and more determined to defend them than they were ever before known or had occasion to be. . . .

Four years later Adams was dining with 350 Sons of Liberty in Dorchester. With Samuel Adams as their patron saint and Paul Revere one of their strongest leaders, the Sons of Liberty was a secret organization formed to enforce disobedience to the Stamp Act. It numbered some prominent men but mostly mechanics and dock workers. It was a strong-arm society, using arson, physical violence, and tar and feathers to persuade the recalcitrant to its views.

Divided Society

In Boston, the upper classes were mostly Tory and Loyalist. Crown officials and those connected with them were naturally pro-Britain. Church of England clergymen were loyal to the crown to which they owed their denominational fealty. Most of Boston's merchants were Loyalists. Much of their wealth depended on trade with England where their connections were firm. Prominent physicians who had studied in England were Loyalists.

Most of the Congregational clergy, with their inherited belief in the separate and sacrosanct Holy Commonwealth of Massachusetts Bay, were Whigs. The bulk of the working class sided with the Whigs, as did the dockers, apprentices, and town toughs. They had nothing to lose, and they enjoyed the furies of unleashed destruction and the free liquor provided by those who incited them to ever-greater violence.

Party lines were not, of course, drawn this sharply. Many leading lawyers were Tories, while others, such as John Adams, were Whigs. Scenting chances of great profit or, like John Hancock, smarting under prosecution, some merchants were Whigs and thus Separatists.

Unlike their Boston counterparts, the country gentry were largely Whig. They were the large landholders, the shrewd traders. They owed their local leadership to holding town offices and to command in the militia. The country people, who looked up to these squires, followed their lead.

There were generations of farmers in western Massachusetts who had never known England. Their country was the village in which they lived and the land they tilled. Their fellow countrymen were not English but "New English." The policing British regulars in Boston whom they heard about were the hirelings of a foreign power. Patriotism was born of the feeling all these things aroused. Men's loyalties are not ordinarily governed by their political beliefs but by their feelings.

In the opinion of John Adams, about one-third of the American colonists were Tories, one-third Whig. The other third remained uncommitted.

In Massachusetts, there were other aspects to the emotions which first expressed themselves in complaint, then in violent disobedience, then in outright war. In many ways this was a rising of the lower classes against the class in power. It was a rebellion of the ruled against the entrenched authority of their rulers. To some extent it was youth and vitality against age and discipline—John Adams was almost a quarter century younger than Thomas Hutchinson. There were economic causes—Massachusetts clamored for the right to do business as it wished anywhere in the world.

The Boston Mob

The Boston mob was a fearful engine. Excited and incited by such men as Samuel Adams, sailors and vagrants joined the apprentices and toughs in orgies of brutality and vengeance. Many suffered the mob's attention. One suffered more than most.

Thomas Hutchinson had just returned the evening of August 26, 1765, from his country home in Milton when the mob attacked his mansion. Hutchinson, whom they sought to murder, directed his children to a place of safety. He locked the house and determined to stand his ground. Only when his eldest daughter returned and refused to leave without him did he go with her to a neighbor's.

The mob intended to level Hutchinson's house to the ground. They destroyed the cupola and part of the roof but could not knock down the brick walls. Senseless vandalism continued all night as they wrecked the interior of the fine home with axes. They tore down hangings, ruined paneling, carted off furniture, and stole nine hundred pounds. They destroyed Hutchinson's invaluable library, strewed his carefully collected documents and notes about the street, and carted off the manuscript of the second volume of his *History of the Colony and Province of Massachusetts-Bay*. The Rev. John Eliot, a neighbor, rescued what papers he could. The damage done by the mob was officially estimated at over three thousand pounds.

Thomas Hutchinson disapproved most of the major measures against which the Whigs protested, but embittered by this barbarism, he was more than ever determined to enforce England's laws to the letter.

He had little chance of success. The dice of the gods were loaded against Thomas Hutchinson now, for there was another force in Massachusetts. The province had inherited the dictatorial spirit of its early clergy and politicians. Though their vocabulary had changed, its people still distinguished between what they were certain was of God and what of the devil. The Whigs were as certain of their righteousness in fighting England as their forebears had been in hanging witches or selling Indians into slavery in Africa. Sober conservatism had little chance against the fiery oratory of Otis, the inflammatory propaganda of Samuel Adams, or the strong will and judgment of John Adams.

Massachusetts provoked the first skirmishes on the Boston streets, saw the first armed clashes between British troops and American forces, and fought the first major engagement of the Revolutionary War. The temper of its aroused populace, the repressive actions of the provincial government, and the determined resistance of the Sons of Liberty made the outbreak inevitable.

The Boston Massacre

On March 5, 1770, a Boston mob began to taunt the soldiers on guard in King Street, throwing stones and daring the frightened soldiers to fire on them. To avoid trouble, an officer ordered the men back into their barracks, and the alarm bell was rung. The crowd then shouted that it would kill a sentry on duty at the Customs House. He raised his gun and called for help. A captain and a squad came on the double from the Town House. The jeering crowd pelted them with stones and jeering cries of, "Fire! Fire!" In the confusion the tormented soldiers thought they heard the order. They fired into the crowd, killing three and wounding six.

Faneuil Hall was a public market and hall given to Boston by merchant Peter Faneuil in 1742

The leader of the men slain, thus an early hero of the American cause, was a giant Negro of about 47 years of age. His name was Crispus Attucks. He is thought to have been a runaway slave who had been the property of William Browne of Framingham who advertised for the recovery of a slave named "Crispus" in the *Boston Gazette* in November 1750. Immortalized in Paul Revere's well-known engraving of the action in which he met his death, Crispus Attucks is sometimes said to have been a sailor on a whaling ship, sometimes described as a worker in the Boston ropewalk.

The "Boston Massacre," as the inspired Samuel Adams quickly described it, was a street brawl started by rioters, but it was a heaven-sent gift to the patriot cause. Adams convinced Boston that it was the cold-blooded slaying by British hirelings of innocent Bostonians. At a packed meeting in Faneuil Hall the next day he roared for vengeance.

The slain were given heroes' funerals and interred in the Old Granary Burial Grounds. Samuel Adams argued before Hutchinson that the British soldiers and the citizens of Boston could not live together. Hutchinson ordered the soldiers off the Common, where they had been encamped, and into the fort. With John Quincy, John Adams, who was castigated for his fairness, defended the British captain and his men when they were brought to trial. Two enlisted men were found guilty and were branded on the hand. The officer and six men were found innocent and freed.

Paul Revere made an engraving of the Boston Massacre which showed a line of British soldiers drawn up in battle array deliberately mowing down a cowering and helpless crowd. On March 5 of each year, bells tolled mournfully. At night, lighted pictures of the martyrs were paraded through the streets, and some prominent Whig gave a commemorative harangue. In 1772, Dr. Joseph Warren cried out that the soldiers had "promiscuously scattered death among the innocent inhabitants of a populous city."

The Boston Tea Party

Massachusetts placed an embargo on all British goods. As a result, British merchants suffered badly. The Townshend Acts had been repealed, but not the tax on tea. The East India Company had tea piling up in its warehouses in England. It persuaded Parliament to let it ship out this tea without paying duty in England, planning to collect the duty in American ports where it could sell the tea cheaply.

Boston would not accept the tea, objecting to the tax of threepence per pound. There was another objection. The bulk of the tea was consigned to Thomas and Elisha Hutchinson, sons of the governor, who hoped to undercut the market and sell the tea at a profit direct to New England consumers.

The *Dartmouth,* first of the three tea ships—the other two were the *Eleanor* and the *Beaver*—docked in Boston on Sunday, November 8, 1773. Its captain was made to promise that he would not unload until the following Tuesday. Boston's Whig newspapers denounced the taxed tea and urged strong measures. The nearby towns were alerted. A huge mass meeting was called in Faneuil Hall. There was an impasse. The patriots would not pay the tax; Governor

Hutchinson would not clear the three ships out of Boston harbor until the tax had been paid and the tea unloaded.

So large was the protest meeting that it had to be moved to the Old South Church, where seven thousand jammed the meeting house or milled about outside. The captain of the *Dartmouth* reported that the governor still would not yield. "This meeting can do no more to save the country!" shouted Samuel Adams. At his words, thirty to sixty men—accounts differ—dressed as "Mohock" Indians rushed down to Griffin's Wharf, hacked open all the chests of tea on all three ships with their hatchet-tomahawks and dumped it into the harbor. They were surrounded by armed British ships, but none interfered.

Even sober John Adams said that the Boston Tea Party was the grandest thing that had happened since the controversy with England began.

Retaliation

To punish Boston for this flagrant destruction and the loss of eighteen thousand pounds worth of tea Parliament passed the "Coercive Acts." One of these closed the port of Boston. Ships were immobilized. Merchants could no longer do business. Carters, dockers, longshoremen, and sailors were thrown out of work. Farmers no longer had a market to which they could take their produce.

The boycott of British goods was rigidly enforced. You could buy if you wished, but then the Sons of Liberty would come and burn your house down or tar and feather you. You might get hanged in effigy or, if the crowd got too excited and made a slight error, in person.

Parliament declared Massachusetts in a state of rebellion and imposed martial law. Crack troops of the British army were sent to enforce it. The barracks and the fort could not hold them all so hated "lobsterbacks" were billeted on protesting Boston families.

Anger mounted to fury. Fiery pamphlets and newspaper articles denounced England's Parliament, the King, and all oppression.

The Massachusetts Spy

Strongest propaganda arm of the Whigs was now *The Massachusetts Spy* which the Boston printer, Isaiah Thomas, founded in 1770. Despite threats of libel and of personal violence, Thomas made the *Spy* office what the Tories angrily called a sedition foundry. He defied his enemies and called loudly for independence. A *Spy* piece, October 8, 1771, closed:

> Should the liberty of the press be once destroyed, farewell the remainder of our valuable rights and privileges! We may next expect padlocks on our lips, fetters on our legs, and only our hands left at liberty to slave for *our worse than Egyptian taskmasters*, or—or—FIGHT OUR WAY TO CONSTITUTIONAL FREEDOM.

In 1774, adopting a device which he did not originate, Thomas printed a snake divided into nine parts across the top of the *Spy*. One part was for all New England, the other parts were for the remaining colonies. Over the snake was "JOIN OR DIE." With Samuel Adams and John Hancock, Isaiah Thomas was placed on the list of those to be summarily executed if captured. He got himself and his press out of Boston, across the Charles River, and to Worcester in April 1775—just in time.

Lexington and Concord

Paul Revere made the gallop celebrated by Longfellow the night of the eighteenth of that month. The next day, British regulars marched from Boston to destroy American military stores in Concord and to capture Samuel Adams and Hancock, who were in hiding in Lexington. After an initial skirmish in Lexington they met a force of about five hundred hastily aroused "Minutemen" at Concord Bridge. Both British and Americans died in the brief battle where, Emerson wrote in 1836, "the embattled farmers stood and fired the shot heard round the world."

The first blood of what became the American Revolution was shed in Lexington, April 19, 1775

The British destroyed the arms and ammunition in Concord but were harried back to Boston. Fighting and marching in battle order, they could not cope with the guerrilla tactics of the colonials. Their withdrawal became a retreat.

Massachusetts had sent John Adams and Samuel Adams to the First Continental Congress the preceding September, friends buying Samuel Adams clothes and supplying him with money for the journey. Oddly, John Adams was sent in place of Major Joseph Hawley of Northampton, who was unable to go because of ill health. (Hawley, who was Jonathan Edwards' cousin and enemy, went insane in 1776.)

Massachusetts' delegates to the Second Continental Congress were John and Samuel Adams, Thomas Cushing, Robert Treat Paine, and James Bowdoin. It was John Adams, with Samuel Adams seconding the motion, who nominated George Washington for commander-in-chief of the American forces. Those forces had been gathering about Boston.

159

Bunker Hill

Bunker Hill in Charlestown commanded the city and the harbor. The night of June 16, 1775, about eight hundred colonial troops were sent to fortify the hill. By morning they had built an earthworks across Breed's Hill—lower than Bunker Hill and nearer the Bay—and were extending breastworks across the Charlestown peninsula.

In the battle which took place that afternoon some two thousand British regulars attacked about half that number of Massachusetts colonials. The British infantry, each man carrying 125 pounds of equipment, advanced uphill in battle order; the colonials waited behind their protective breastworks.

Colonel William Prescott issued his famous order: "Don't fire until you see the white of their eyes!"

The Americans held their fire until the British were only fifty feet away. Then they opened a merciless fire. The British were twice driven back but re-formed and came on, always in precise order,

Old print of the engagement at the South Bridge in Concord. The Provincials were headed by Colonel Robinson and Major Buttrick

offering perfect targets. They took Bunker Hill in a costly victory, one the English commanders did not care to repeat. The Americans lost between four and five hundred men, among them Dr. Joseph Warren. The British lost more than a thousand, including ninety officers.

The battle was still raging, June 18, 1775, when Abigail Adams wrote her husband in Philadelphia.

> Dearest Friend.
> Charlestown is laid in ashes. The battle began upon our intrenchments upon Bunker's Hill, Saturday morning about three o'clock, and has not eased yet, and it is now three o'clock Sabbath afternoon. . . . How many have fallen we know not. The constant roar of the cannon is so distressing, that we cannot eat, drink, or sleep. I shall tarry here till it is thought unsafe by my friends and then I have secured myself a retreat at your brother's, who has kindly offered me part of his house. I cannot compose myself to write any further at present.

Evacuation of Boston

General Viscount William Howe, sent to replace Thomas Gage, had both a strong fleet and about eleven hundred trained men in Boston. George Washington, who took the oath as commander-in-

chief in the Harvard Yard, July 2, 1775, set up his headquarters in Cambridge, and his forces were just outside the city. The British were almost on a beleaguered island.

Crowded with Loyalists who had fled into the city for protection, Boston waited. Washington drilled his mechanics and farmers, shaping them into an army. The British were well supplied from the sea. There were just a few inconveniences. Firewood was in short supply, but they tore down houses—one of them John Winthrop's —for fuel, and turned the Old South Meeting House into a cavalry riding school.

Howe did not wish to risk another Bunker Hill. The winter passed in watchful waiting. Washington, who had been unwilling to risk his raw force against the entrenched British, moved in the spring. On March 4, 1776, he took and fortified Dorchester Heights, which overlooked Boston from the mainland, and began to shell the city. There was no counterfire. After a few days, Howe sent officers under a flag of truce to tell Washington that he intended to withdraw. The British and their American adherents abandoned Boston on March 17, 1776, and Washington and his men moved in.

Over two thousand Loyalists fled with Howe, among them some of the wealthiest and most aristocratic families in Massachusetts. About eleven hundred of them, including the Chief Justice, over two hundred merchants, even some mechanics and farmers, sailed to Halifax with the British. Their property was confiscated by the exultant patriots.

Loyalists and those suspected of being Loyalists were forced to swear that they believed the war just and necessary. If they could not satisfy the new authorities of their patriotism, they were forced to give up their arms and ammunition. They could not vote or hold office. Salaries of ministers and teachers who refused to subscribe to the revolutionary cause were immediately stopped. Anyone who had assisted the British or taken refuge inside their lines was disenfranchised.

October 16, 1778, the General Court ordered the arrest and deportation of a long list of Massachusetts men should they return. If they returned a second time, they would be executed. On the list were provincial officials, lawyers, many merchants, cabinetmakers, printers, tallow chandlers, physicians, laborers, "gentlemen," and men of other trades and professions or of none. One name led all the rest. He was "Thomas Hutchinson, Esq., formerly governor of this state."

Hutchinson had obtained permission to go to England in 1774, General Gage being made governor *pro tem* until his return. Events precluded his coming back. In England he worked on a third volume of his history, was awarded an honorary degree by Oxford—and longed to go home. His property confiscated, he was forced to live on the bounty of the king he had tried so stoutly to serve. Homesick to the last, he died in England in 1780.

In Philadelphia

John Hancock, who had been president of the Provincial Congress of Massachusetts, was elected president of the Second Continental Congress, but the Massachusetts delegates were suspect as radical and reckless. Massachusetts had started the war; it had provoked the Coercive Acts. Samuel Adams had fomented insurrection everywhere. It was Massachusetts which England had declared in a state of rebellion. Why should the others colonies help pay with men and money for Massachusetts' rashness?

The delegates from the various colonies, most of them lawyers, were all liberals, but they were cautious and thoughtful men. At first most of them had no wish to separate from England. They were his majesty's loyal if vigorously protesting opposition. What they asked was reform and fairer treatment. They sought conciliation and distrusted the Massachusetts men who were out for blood.

Sectional interests had to be satisfied and jealousies appeased. It was to gain the support of Virginia that the Adamses backed George

Washington to lead the colonial forces. John Hancock, who had no qualification for it, wanted the job himself and did not forgive the action of his colleagues.

The idea of political independence of Great Britain came slowly in the Continental Congress. When it did come, it gathered momentum rapidly. In June 1776, a committee was appointed to draft a proclamation announcing the separation of the thirteen American colonies from Great Britain. The action was greatly stimulated by publication of Thomas Paine's *Common Sense*, but there was more to it than that. Actually England had been more lenient with her colonies in North America than Spain and France with theirs, but democratic sentiment was rising in Europe. Imperialism was already on the wane. From the long view of history, the American colonies simply obtained their freedom from the British Empire a comparatively few years before India and the colonies in Africa obtained theirs.

There was also a practical and expedient side to the matter. As the always shrewd Franklin remarked at the time, they all had to hang together or hang separately. Thomas Jefferson wrote the Declaration of Independence, submitted it first to Franklin and John Adams, then to the Congress. Adams pushed it through. "He was our colossus on the floor," Jefferson said. Adopted by the Congress, July 4, 1776, it was read to the people from the State House in Boston on July 18.

The Revolution had been a fact in Massachusetts long before it was formally announced as a political theory. Massachusetts men fought throughout the war in many battles in many places. Thousands of Massachusetts seamen sailed on privateers out of Boston, Salem, Ipswich, Beverly, Newburyport, Gloucester, and Marblehead. Massachusetts even had a state navy of fifteen ships. Massachusetts bore a large share of the expense of the war.

Yet after Washington's seizure of Boston the actual war went elsewhere. Boston's blockaded port lay idle; its ships rotted at anchor.

164

General Howe ordered that all cannon that could not be taken from Boston should be thrown into the harbor. Carelessly spiked, many of these guns were later repaired and used by the Americans. One Tory wrote that the evacuating ships were so crowded that everyone was "obliged to pig together on the floor"

The city's population fell from about twenty-five thousand to about ten thousand. Exhausted by its early efforts, the depleted city did not begin to regain its vigor and importance until the long war's end.

The Massachusetts Constitution

As early as May 1776, the Continental Congress had recommended that each of the thirteen confederated colonies draw up a state constitution. Massachusetts was the last to comply.

After the overthrow of British provincial authority it governed itself under its old charter. Then western Massachusetts began to demand a written constitution for Massachusetts. Accordingly, in June 1777, the General Court appointed a committee to draft one, and the Court accepted the draft which it prepared. The constitution was then submitted to the towns. It was rejected by a large vote.

The rejection stemmed largely from objections raised by Theophilus Parsons, a Newburyport lawyer who later became chief justice of the state. Because they emanated from a meeting of delegates from that county, they were set forth in a pamphlet called the "Essex Result." In this, Parsons insisted that the proposed constitution draw a firm line between judicial and executive authority. He asked a system of checks and balances with a government in three distinct parts: executive, judicial, and legislative. He advocated a legislature of two houses, one with greater authority than the other, and a guarantee of religious freedom.

To consider these objections and recommendations, a constitutional convention was called. In September 1779, three hundred delegates representing Massachusetts towns gathered in the meeting house of the First Church in Cambridge, James Bowdoin presiding. A committee of twenty-seven men was appointed to write the constitution. It delegated the responsibility to three of its members. As usual, one man did the work. The man was John Adams.

The best legal mind in Massachusetts public life, Adams had widened his Congressional experience with service as envoy in France. He drew up a constitution of thirty-one articles, twenty-seven of which were accepted after debate in the convention. Adams returned to France; his constitution, with an explanatory "Address of the Convention," was submitted to the towns. It was approved by the necessary two-thirds majority of the voters.

June 16, 1780, James Bowdoin announced that the Massachusetts constitution—which served as a model for the United States Constitution of 1787—had been adopted. It went into effect October 25, 1780, when, by a large majority, John Hancock was elected the first governor of the commonwealth.

Just one hundred sixty years after the *Mayflower* reached Plymouth and exactly a century and a half after the Puritans founded Boston, the Commonwealth of Massachusetts, which their coming had presaged, was established.

Bibliography

Adams, James Truslow, *The Founding of New England*. Boston: The Atlantic Monthly Press, 1921.

Andrews, Charles M., *Colonial Folkways*. New Haven: Yale University Press, 1919.

Beard, Charles A. and Mary R., *The Rise of American Civilization*. New York: The Macmillan Co., 1930.

Bradford, William, *Of Plymouth Plantation, 1620-1647*, intro. by Samuel Eliot Morison. New York: Alfred A. Knopf, 1952.

Dictionary of American Biography, centenary edition. New York: Charles Scribner's Sons, 1946.

Dow, George Francis, *Domestic Life in New England in the Seventeenth Century*. Topsfield, Mass.: The Perkins Press, 1925.

Duyckinck, Evert A. and George L., eds., *Cyclopedia of American Literature*, 2 vols. New York: Charles Scribner, 1866.

Elliott, Charles W., *The New England History*, 2 vols. New York: Charles Scribner, 1857.

Faulkner, Harold Underwood, *American Economic History*, 9th ed. New York: Harper & Bros., 1943.

Fiske, John, *The Beginnings of New England*. Boston: Houghton, Mifflin and Co., 1889.

Greene, Evarts Boutell, *The Revolutionary Generation*. New York: The Macmillan Co., 1943.

Hart, Albert Bushnell, ed., *Commonwealth History of Massachusetts*, 5 vols. New York: The States History Co., 1927-1928.

Hawthorne, Julian, *The History of the United States*, 3 vols. New York: P. F. Collier & Son, 1912.

Holland, Josiah Gilbert, *History of Western Massachusetts*, 2 vols. Springfield: Samuel Bowles and Co., 1855.

Howe, Henry F., *Early Explorers of Plymouth Harbor, 1525-1619*. Plymouth: Plimoth Plantation, Inc., and the Pilgrim Society, 1953.

Hutchinson, Thomas, *The History of the Colony and Province of Massachusetts-Bay*, 2 vols., ed. by Lawrence Shaw Mayo. Cambridge: Harvard University Press, 1936.

Johnson, Edward, *The Wonder-Working Providence, 1638-1651*, ed. by J. Franklin Jameson. New York: Barnes & Noble, 1937.

Judd, Sylvester, *History of Hadley*. Northampton: Metcalf & Co., 1863.

——— "The Judd Manuscript," vols. 1-5. Forbes Library, Northampton, Mass.

Langdon, William Chauncey, *Everyday Things in American Life*, 2 vols. New York: Charles Scribner's Sons, 1937, 1941.

Lodge, Henry Cabot, *Boston*. New York: Longmans, Green & Co., 1891.

Mather, Cotton, *Magnalia Christi Americana*, 2 vols. Hartford: Silas Andrus & Sons, 1853.

167

Morison, Samuel Eliot, *Builders of the Bay Colony*. Boston: Houghton Mifflin Co., 1930.

———— *The Story of the "Old Colony" of New Plymouth*. New York: Alfred A. Knopf, 1956.

Mourt's Relation: A Journal of the Pilgrims at Plymouth, ed. by Dwight B. Heath. New York: Corinth Books, n.d., originally published 1622.

Powell, Sumner Chilton, *Puritan Village*. New York: Doubleday & Co., 1965.

Sanderlin, George, *1776: Journals of American Independence*. New York: Harper & Row, 1968.

Starkey, Marion L., *The Devil in Massachusetts*. New York: Alfred A. Knopf, 1949.

Trent, William P., and Wells, Benjamin W., eds., *Colonial Prose and Poetry*, 3 vols. New York: Thomas Y. Crowell Co., 1901, 1903.

Trumbull, James Russell, *History of Northampton, Massachusetts, from its Settlement in 1654*, 2 vols. Northampton: Press of the Gazette Publishing Co., 1898.

Tunis, Edwin, *Colonial Craftsmen and the Beginnings of American Industry*. Cleveland: The World Publishing Co., 1965.

Wertenbaker, Thomas Jefferson, *The First Americans, 1607-1690*. New York: The Macmillan Co., 1927.

Winsor, Justin, ed., *The Memorial History of Boston*, 4 vols. Boston: James R. Osgood and Co., 1882.

Winthrop, John, *The History of New England, 1630-1649*, 2 vols., ed. by James K. Hosmer. New York: Barnes & Noble, 1959.

Wissler, Clark, *Indians of the United States: Four Centuries of Their History and Culture*, rev. ed. New York: Doubleday & Co., 1966.

Wood, James Playsted, *Boston*. New York: The Seabury Press, 1967.

———— *Mr. Jonathan Edwards*. New York: The Seabury Press, 1968.

———— *The Story of Advertising*. New York: The Ronald Press Co., 1958.

Important Dates

c.1001	Leif Eiriksson lands on Cape Cod, and Norsemen try to establish a settlement at Vinland during the next few years
1602	Bartholomew Gosnold sails to Cape Cod, Martha's Vineyard, and Buzzards Bay
1603	Under Martin Pring's command, the *Speedwell* and *Discoverer* dock in Plymouth harbor
1614	Captain John Smith explores and maps the Massachusetts coast
1620	Pilgrims draw up Mayflower Compact and settle Plymouth
1628	Governor and Company of the Massachusetts Bay granted a charter
1629	Puritans settle Salem
1630	Boston is settled and becomes the capital of Massachusetts Bay
1634	Boston Latin School instituted
1636	Harvard College established
	The Connecticut Valley opened for settlement
	The Pequot War provokes more Indian hostilities
1643	Colonies of Massachusetts Bay, Plymouth, Connecticut, and New Haven form the New England Confederation for mutual safety
1675–6	Indians gain revenge in King Philip's War for indignities suffered at the hands of the colonists
1684	England invalidates the charter of 1628 and appoints Joseph Dudley provisional governor
1690–1760	French and Indian Wars are fought for the survival of both England and Massachusetts
1691	King William III signs new charter for the Province of Massachusetts Bay
1692	Salem witchcraft trials
1740	The "Great Awakening" temporarily fires Massachusetts with religious fanaticism
1765	The Stamp Act touches off patriotic protests

1770	Boston objects to the tax on tea
	March 5, the Boston Massacre inspires the patriots' cause
1773	December 16, Patriots dress as Indians and dump tea into the harbor at the Boston Tea Party
1774	Coercive Acts close the port of Boston
	First Provincial Congress meets
1775	Second Provincial Congress nominates George Washington as commander in chief of American forces
	April 19, skirmish at Lexington and battle at Concord Bridge
	June 17, Battle of Bunker Hill brings a costly victory to the British
1776	March 17, General Howe and the British evacuate Boston
	July 4, Declaration of Independence is adopted by the Congress
1780	October 25, First Massachusetts constitution becomes effective
	John Hancock is elected first governor of the commonwealth

Historic Sites

BOSTON. A walking tour approximately 1½ miles long begins at Boston Common and takes in fifteen colonial shrines of Massachusetts. Among them are the *Park Street Church, Granary Burying Ground, King's Chapel, Old Corner Bookstore, Old South Meeting House, Old State House, Boston Massacre Site, Faneuil Hall, Paul Revere House,* and *Old North Church.* Freedom Trail Information Booth at Lafayette Mall on Tremont Street by Boston Common. Just off the trail are the *Bunker Hill Monument,* and *Copp's Hill Burying Ground,* where Increase and Cotton Mather are buried

CAMBRIDGE, just north across the Charles River from Boston. Site of the country's oldest college, Harvard, and the headquarters of Washington during the Revolution (later Longfellow's home)

CONCORD, nineteen miles northwest of Boston just off Mass. 2. *Minute Man National Historical Park* includes the *Old North Bridge,* where the Revolution began in April, 1775, as well as the *Buttrick Mansion, Minute Man Statue* and the *Old Manse.* Other points of interest nearby are the *Wright Tavern, Hill Burying Ground*, and the *Antiquarian Museum*

LEXINGTON, just north of Boston on Mass. 225. The *Minute Man Statue* on the "Green" marks the first skirmish of British and colonial forces. Built in 1690, the *Old Buckman Tavern* was the rallying point for Lexington militiamen. *Munroe Tavern*, erected in 1697, was used as a British hospital and contains relics of Revolutionary days

OLD DEERFIELD VILLAGE, off U.S. 5, about thirty miles north of Springfield. A mile-long street of restored colonial homes, and an Indian Museum

OLD STURBRIDGE VILLAGE, near the intersection of Mass. 15 and 20. A complete reproduction of a New England village of 1800, with houses, shops, school, gardens, cattle pound, a working farm, and other exhibits, but many of the buildings and some of their contents date from the earlier colonial period. Facsimile copies of *The Massachusetts Spy* are printed in Isaiah Thomas's printing office which is now in the village

PLYMOUTH, off Mass. 3A on the west coast of Cape Cod Bay. In downtown Plymouth are *Plymouth Rock* and *Mayflower II*, a reproduction which sailed across the Atlantic from England in 1957, and *Forefathers' Monument*. Two miles south on 3A is *Plimoth Plantation*, the Pilgrims' village of 1627. Replicas of the homes of Bradford, Brewster, Standish, Alden, and a common house, a sawpit, herb gardens, and the fort-meeting house can be seen today. *Pilgrim Hall* exhibits many of the actual possessions of the Pilgrims

PROVINCETOWN, at the end of Cape Cod off U.S. 6. *Pilgrim Monument* commemorates the landing of the first Pilgrims after their voyage of sixty-five days across the ocean

QUINCY, just south of Boston off Mass. 3A. The *John Adams House* and the *John Quincy Adams House* are located here. The *Old House* contains Adams furniture and memorabilia. The *Quincy Homestead*, at Hancock St. and Butler Rd., is a restored and furnished monument of colonial times

SALEM, on Mass. 1A about fifteen miles north of Boston. Historic Trail covers *Pioneer Village*, a reproduction of the buildings the early settlers erected; *Witch House*, dating from 1675, the restored home of Jonathan Corwin, judge of the Witchcraft Court; *John Ward*

171

House, one of the most unspoiled of early New England houses, built in 1684; *Ropes Mansion,* 1719; and the *House of the Seven Gables,* built in 1668 by John Turner. The Historical Museum of the *Essex Institute* displays furniture, portraits, miniatures, costumes, and decorative arts

SAUGUS IRONWORKS RESTORATION, off U.S. 1 and Mass. 125, at Main Street. The birthplace of America's iron and steel industry appears as it did about 1650 with blast furnace, forge, huge waterwheels, and the ironmaster's house

THE WAYSIDE INN, at Sudbury, off Mass. 20, twenty miles outside Boston. The Inn dates from 1686 and sheltered both Washington and Lafayette. Longfellow later immortalized it

For additional historic sites, consult *New England Museums and Historic Houses,* current edition, published cooperatively by the New England Council, the Museum of Fine Arts, and the Society for the Preservation of New England Antiquities. Free copies are available by contacting the New England Council, Statler Office Bldg., Boston.

For location of Historic Sites, see map on page 3

Index

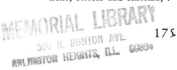

Colonial Histories

The thirteen colonies that formed the nucleus of a new nation in 1776 have a history stretching back to the first settlements almost as long as their record as states of the union. This series of histories on each of the original colonies brings to life the men and events of that formative era. Letters, eyewitness reports, maps, prints, and documents highlight the text. By limiting the scope of the series it has been possible to include the colorful details that make the colonial period vivid. A determined effort has been made to "tell it like it was" on subjects such as treatment of the Indians and indentured servants, slavery, and the hardships many colonists endured. This series is recommended for students, teachers, and the general reader with an interest in America's colonial past.